CONTENTS

- 02
- 04 **WORLD WAR ONE: THE FIRST TANKS**
- 08 **GREAT WAR ANTI-TANK TACTICS**
- 12 **THE TWENTIES AND THIRTIES: EXPERIMENTATION AND A NEW WAR**
- 18 **BLITZKRIEG PANZER**
- 22 **PIAT: THE PANZER KILLER**
- 28 **WORLD WAR TWO: LESSONS FROM THE DESERT WAR**
- 32 **BAZOOKA AND THE SHAPED CHARGE**
- 38 **TANK DEVELOPMENT BY NATION**
- 44 **THE GREATEST LIVE SHOW OF HISTORIC MOVING ARMOUR**
- 46 **NASHORN PHOENIX**
- 50 **WORLD WAR TWO: ARMOURED THRUSTS IN NORTH WEST EUROPE**
- 54 **TANK TERROR: PANZERSCHRECK**
- 60 **RETURN OF THE CENTAUR**
- 68 **COLD WAR: SUSPICION AND STOCKPILING**
- 72 **BAT GUN**
- 76 **THE BRITISH ARMY AND THE FUTURE OF THE TANK**
- 80 **NLAW: THE ULTIMATE TANK KILLER**

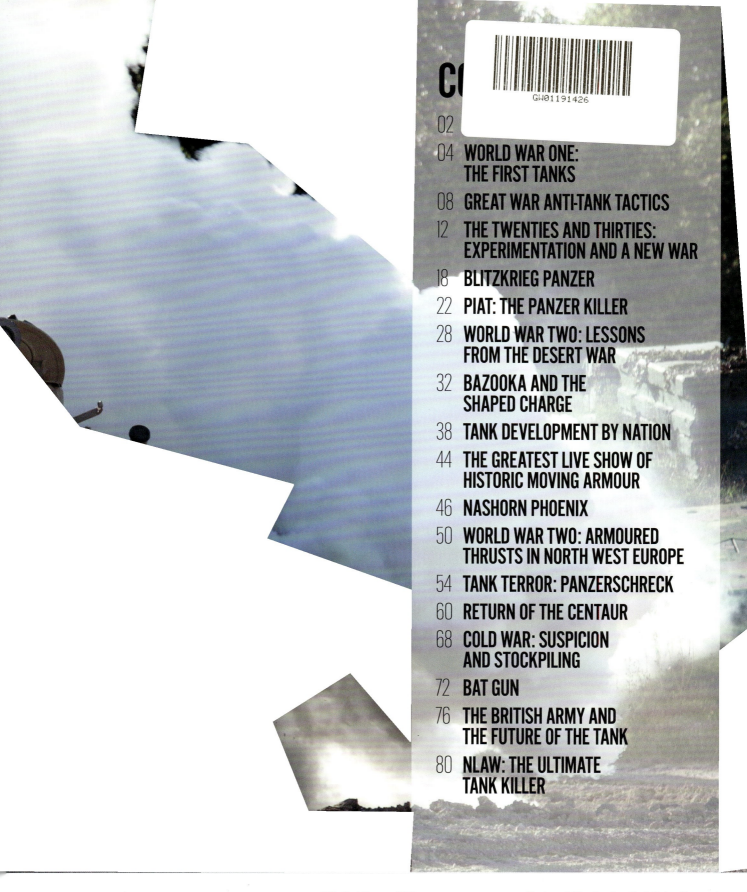

© The Tank Museum 2023
All rights reserved. No part of this publication may be reproduced or stored in a retrieval system or transmitted, in any form or by any means, electronic, mechanical, photocopying, recording or otherwise, without prior permission in writing from The Tank Museum.
ISBN 978-1-739-35472-5

Designed and produced for The Tank Museum by JJN Publishing Ltd.

Production Director: Nigel Clements
Editorial Director: Jonathan Falconer
Art Director: Jud Webb
Photography: Matt Sampson, John St John, Charlie Marsh, Alastair Jennings.

Thanks to: William Bannister, Gavin Barlow/Armoured Engineering, Tim Broad, Chris Copson, Rosanna Dean, Defence Images/Crown Copyright Open License, Ian Hudson, Jose Martinez, Craig Moore/*Classic Military Vehicle* magazine, Robby van Sambeek, Stuart Wheeler, David Willey.

Join us: Support The Tank Museum by finding and following us on all these social media platforms.

TANKFEST SOUVENIR SPECIAL 3

Above: Titans of the Great War battlefield – German A7V, British Mark IV and French Schneider CA1. Below: The Tank Museum's replica Mark IV and A7V – the fear induced by the approach of such machines in battle can be well imagined.

The first action of the German A7V tank on 21 March 1918 is not very well known from the British side. It was a promising start from a nation that would come to lead the world in tank design 20 years later.

IN THE ARENA
WORLD WAR ONE: THE FIRST TANKS

The genesis of the tank, its first use in combat on the Somme in 1916 and the rapid emergence of anti-tank warfare.

Reenactors wearing authentic kit and carrying replica weapons add to the accurate period feel of the arena displays at TANKFEST.

Living History displays are part of the TANKFEST experience.

A pair of French Renault FT tanks with the replica Mark IV. Rather than a large, heavy vehicle, the concept behind the FT was for a small and light tank that would be more manoeuvrable, harder to hit and could be fielded in large numbers.

REPLICA MARK IV

The Tank Museum's running Mark IV is a replica tank built specially for the film *War Horse* by Neil Corbold Special Effects. It was purchased by the museum after filming was complete in 2010. The tank is built around the engine and running gear of an old Hyundai excavator, and a box steel structure was welded together for strength. Mild steel panels and other improvisations make the tank look very authentic in appearance. Having replica vehicles like this means photography, filming and displays are possible in a way that would be too risky with original vehicles, even if they were in running order.

TANKFEST visitors get the opportunity to see the Mark IV in close-up.

'There are 200 track plates on the Mark IV and four bolts holding each one in place.'

TANKFEST

90 SECS WITH
CHRIS COPSON
COMMENTATOR

'No one could fail to be enthused by tanks, being surrounded by such a fabulous collection, particularly at TANKFEST where we have such an amazing collection of moving armour, both from the museum collection and as guest vehicles,' affirms commentator Chris Copson.

Chris's 'day job' job as a Research Officer at The Tank Museum involves researching, scripting and presenting videos for the museum's YouTube channel, which he finds fascinating as it is a relatively new form of museum interpretation. 'Of course, being YouTube, we get feedback that tells us what people think – mostly good, thankfully!' he laughs.

As an historian specialising in the First World War, Chris worked at The Tank Museum as Education Officer for nine years before moving to The Keep Military Museum as Curator in 2014. He also worked as Collections Director at the Haynes International Motor Museum before being drawn back to The Tank Museum.

'My interest in tanks and armoured warfare really comes from working as Education Officer at The Tank Museum earlier in my career and conducting battlefield tours on the Western Front and in Normandy. I was interested prior to coming here, but it has really developed into a bit of an obsession!' concedes Chris.

'As jobs go,' he admits, 'The Tank Museum is the best office in the world!'

ANTI-TANK WEAPONS
GREAT WAR ANTI-TANK TACTICS

The Tank Museum Curator, **David Willey**, examines the weapons and tactics adopted by the Germans to defeat tanks after their first battlefield appearance in 1916.

German attempts to defeat the tank went through a series of phases – urgency followed by declining concern, followed again, after Cambrai, by a renewed urgency, and took a number of forms ranging from grenades, tank traps and blocks, new artillery tactics, new anti-tank weapons or conversions and improvements, to existing weapons, mines and flamethrowers.

The appearance of tanks on the Somme battlefield for the first time in September 1916 was a genuine surprise to the Germans and created in some places Tankschreck, or 'tank horror'. After the initial confused reports from the frontline had been analysed and assessed, the German High Command responded by ordering their own tank, and more urgently created 50 batteries of 'close-combat' artillery numbered from 201 to 250. After experiments the German Army decided that gun calibres of 57mm to 77mm were needed to defeat tanks. In early 1917, a new anti-tank round was developed for the 77mm gun by Krupp that could penetrate 30mm of armour at 3,000m.

The new artillery units were issued with the 77mm field cannon 96 n.A. but with smaller wheels than on the standard gun (1m diameter as opposed to the usual 1.36m). These batteries had no ammunition limbers and had only four horses to pull each gun instead of six. This was because the new batteries were ordered to certain areas of the frontline where the guns were dug into pits and hidden. The guns were to remain there

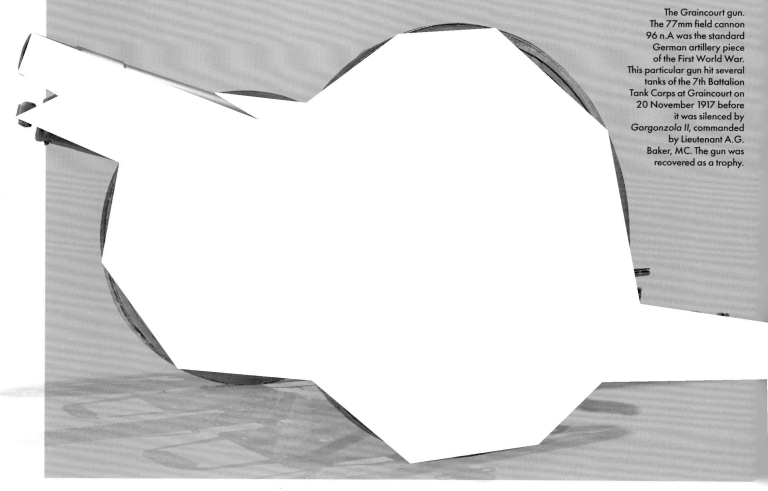

The Graincourt gun. The 77mm field cannon 96 n.A was the standard German artillery piece of the First World War. This particular gun hit several tanks of the 7th Battalion Tank Corps at Graincourt on 20 November 1917 before it was silenced by *Gorgonzola II*, commanded by Lieutenant A.G. Baker, MC. The gun was recovered as a trophy.

8 TANKFEST SOUVENIR SPECIAL

The crew of a Mark V tank inspect a captured T-Gewehr anti-tank rifle at the Battle of Amiens in August 1918.

and not take part in standard artillery engagements such as bombardments and counter-battery work. They were only to be wheeled from their disguised positions to engage with the enemy when attacked by infantry or tanks. Defeating a tank brought monetary rewards – 500 Marks were offered for a tank kill compared to just 150 for bringing down an aeroplane.

Other methods

The German Army had armour-piercing bullets in service before the tank appeared on the battlefield. These 7.92mm SmK bullets fitted their normal rifles and machine-guns, had a chrome nickel steel core, and were designed to penetrate armoured shields used on observation points or by snipers in the trenches. The bullets, however, were difficult to manufacture and never available in the quantities required.

Grenades were sometimes used as demolition or concentrated charges (Gelballte Ladung), and two extra heads wired to a normal grenade was also used to disable tracks or penetrate roofs. Photographs show some clusters with up to eight heads strapped to a single grenade. The chicken-wire netting seen on British Mark I tanks was put in place in anticipation of thrown grenades lodging on the flat roof. Improvisations using similar materials continue to be made on armoured vehicles to this day.

The Germans realised that the K-Flak mobile anti-aircraft batteries could also be used against tanks. The vehicles were made by two manufacturing teams, Krupp and Daimler and Ehrhardt and Rheinmetall, based on a requirement for an 80hp four-wheel-drive vehicle for anti-balloon and aircraft defence. These mainly 77mm anti-aircraft guns, mounted openly on the rear of the trucks, had a fast rate of fire. They were issued with new armour-piercing ammunition, the K Granate 15 P. Their mobility meant they could be quickly brought to an area, as seen at the Battle of Cambrai. The vehicle's success led to other experiments with weapons mounted on trucks and half-tracked vehicles before the end of the war.

Special supports were made for the 7.58cm Minenwerfer or mine-thrower to allow the weapon to be used in an anti-tank role. This small light mortar with a rifled barrel had previously been used in the frontline, with wheels that could be quickly attached to allow it to be dragged

7.7CM FELDKANONE 96 NEUER ART

Manufacturer	Krupp
Production	1905
Total no made	5,086
Weight	1,020kg (2,250lb)
Barrel length	2.080m (6ft 10in) L/27
Width	1.53m (5ft)
Crew	5
Shell	77 x 234mm R or 77 x 227mm R
Shell weight	6.8kg (15lb)
Calibre	77mm (3in)
Breech	Horizontal sliding-wedge
Recoil	Hydro-spring
Carriage	Pole trail
Elevation	-12° 56' to +15° 8'
Traverse	7° 15'
Rate of fire	10 rounds per minute
Muzzle velocity	465m/s (1,530ft/s)
Effective firing range	5,500m (6,000yd)
Maximum firing range	8,400m (9,200yd) with trail dug in.

Lieutenant A.G. Baker MC, 7th Battalion Tank Corps, captured German field guns at Graincourt after driving off their crews, and added a Bar to his MC.

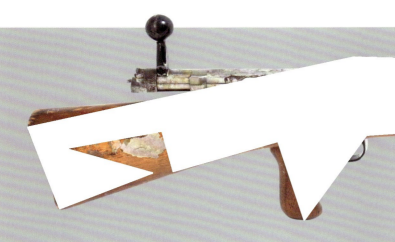

> 'The initial success of tanks at Cambrai reawakened the German High Command to the potency of the new weapon.'

forward to accompany an infantry attack. The new mount added an extended trail, more like an artillery gun, which allowed rounds to be fired directly – on a flat trajectory – at a target up to 1,200m with a 4.6kg round.

'Tankforts' were also designed to be built in areas thought susceptible to tank attack. These could be permanent concrete placements for anti-tank weapons of various calibres or mobile armour-plated pillboxes called a '*Panzerkuppel*'. These housed a 5.7cm quick-firing gun and could be moved into position on a special carriage.

Flammenwerfer
A considerable number of photographs exist and are often reproduced showing German soldiers training with flame-throwers as an anti-tank weapon. The

The 77mm K-Flakwagen. Its mobility was restricted to roads but with the new armour-piercing round it was a potent anti-tank weapon.

An experimental half-track vehicle made by Daimler in late 1918. Fitted with a 37mm naval gun the vehicle was designed to provide more cross-country flexibility than the wheeled K-Flakwagen.

Flammenwerfer came in a number of sizes: the 'Grof' was the largest, a static system that held 100 litres of oil, which could propel flame out to 45m for a 1-minute duration; the 'Kleif' was a man-portable cylinder that carried 10 litres of oil and a lower section with compressed gas to project the oil. A second operator held the hose that projected the flame up to 29m for a 5-second duration; the 'Wex' was the more familiar double doughnut-shaped backpack with the outer ring carrying the oil and the inner the compressed gas. One man could carry and operate this system, jetting flame up to 18m. All these systems meant troops had to wait until a tank was remarkably close before operation.

Traps and blocks
One of the simplest ways to disable an approaching tank was to dig a pit to trap it. Pits or traps were hidden with covering nets or branches and turf: 4m deep by 4m wide was considered ideal. Sometimes mines were placed at the bottom of the pits or they were filled with water to drown the engine. The width of trenches was also considered and the High Command thought 2.5m-wide trenches would prove an obstacle to tanks crossing without assistance.

On roads, concrete blocks were positioned or logs or girders sunk into the road to form a barrier. Near Verdun the Germans threaded steel cable between blocks to create a heavy-duty fence line to protect against tanks. Initially the Germans improvised mines from existing ammunition such as artillery shells or mortar rounds. These were placed in the ground, sometimes covered with a board or plank to increase the pressure area. The usual fuse was replaced by a Druckzunder or pressure fuse. Generally, a charge of 12 to 25kg was needed to effectively destroy a tank.

Misleading assumptions
The urgency to find methods to defeat tanks lessened in 1917 as the Germans saw failed tank attacks at Arras and Bullecourt. Here mud and shellfire meant the tanks had little immediate impact on the course of the battles. During these spring conflicts a number of training tanks, including D26, a Mark II Male, were pressed into the fray (another such tank that saw action at this time, *Flying Scotsman*, now resides in The Tank Museum). A training tank had 'soft' steel plates, not heat-treated armour plate. D26 was knocked out in German-held territory and was subsequently inspected and photographed by the enemy. As their standard SmK ammunition had easily penetrated the armour (the Germans not knowing this was an unarmoured training tank) and other tanks had been disabled by shellfire, the German High Command relaxed their own anti-tank activities and tank-making programme. The first use of French tanks in April in the Chemin des

Dames only reinforced the German confidence as Schneider vehicles suffered high losses. Lulled into a false sense of security, in May 1917 the new special artillery batteries were disbanded.

Despite the use of Mark IV tanks in Flanders later in the year and the capture of an example, the German Army failed to realise the armour was thicker and generally bulletproof against standard rifle and SmK ammunition.

The A7V

The initial success of the tanks at Cambrai in November 1917 reawakened the German High Command to the potency of the new weapon. Captured Mark IV vehicles were assembled to be reused by new German tank units. The A7V (Allgemeine Kriegs-Department 7 Abteilung Verkehrswesen or General War Department 7, Traffic Section) was designed by Joseph Vollmer (1871–1955) in early 1917. After the First World War, Vollmer went on to work in Czechoslovakia and Sweden and is perhaps one of the great 'unknowns' of tank development. The A7V chassis were constructed first, but the lessening threat of Allied tanks meant the tank-building programme dropped in priority. Only after Cambrai was armour plate made available for the completion of the first ten A7Vs in December 1917. They were used in combat in March 1918 and the first tank-versus-tank engagement took place at Villers-Bretonneux in April. The anti-tank capability of the vehicle had few practical opportunities to demonstrate its potential in the First World War.

T-Gewehr

The German Army Headquarters had ordered a new

MAUSER TANKGEWEHR M1918 ANTI-TANK RIFLE

Manufacturer	Mauser
Produced	January 1918–April 1919
Total no made	16,900
Weight	15.9kg (35lb), 18.5kg (41lb) loaded, with bipod
Overall length	169.1cm (5ft 7in)
Barrel length	98.4cm (3ft 2in)
Crew	2
Cartridge	13.2 x 92mm TuF (Tank und Flieger)
Calibre	13.2mm (0.525in)
Action	Bolt action
Rate of fire	Single shot, c.10 rounds per minute
Effective firing range	500m (547yds)
Feed system	Manual
Sights	1,000–5,000m (1,100–5,500yds) notched V

anti-tank rifle in October 1917. The successes of the tanks at Cambrai speeded up production but the new Tankgewehr rifle (or T-Gewehr) did not see widespread use until much later in 1918. The gun was a 13.2mm single-shot rifle of impressive size. Some 15,800 of the guns had been made by the Armistice but they were not popular with the troops. The recoil was considerable and even with a well-aimed and successfully penetrating shot a tank might still not be disabled as the small round might not hit a critical component. This problem was amply demonstrated at a test in September 1918 when 18 rounds were fired at a captured Mark IV, none of which were thought to have effectively knocked the tank out.

A high number of other anti-tank weapons were being tested in 1918 for potential production and use in 1919, including a machine-gun to fire the 13mm rounds of the Tankgewehr. However, the defeat of the German armies in the latter half of 1918 and the Treaty of Versailles brought brought an end to these developments.

New Zealand soldiers examine a German A7V tank nicknamed *Schnuck*, captured by New Zealand forces on the Western Front. The photograph was taken on 8 September 1918 by Henry Armytage Sanders.

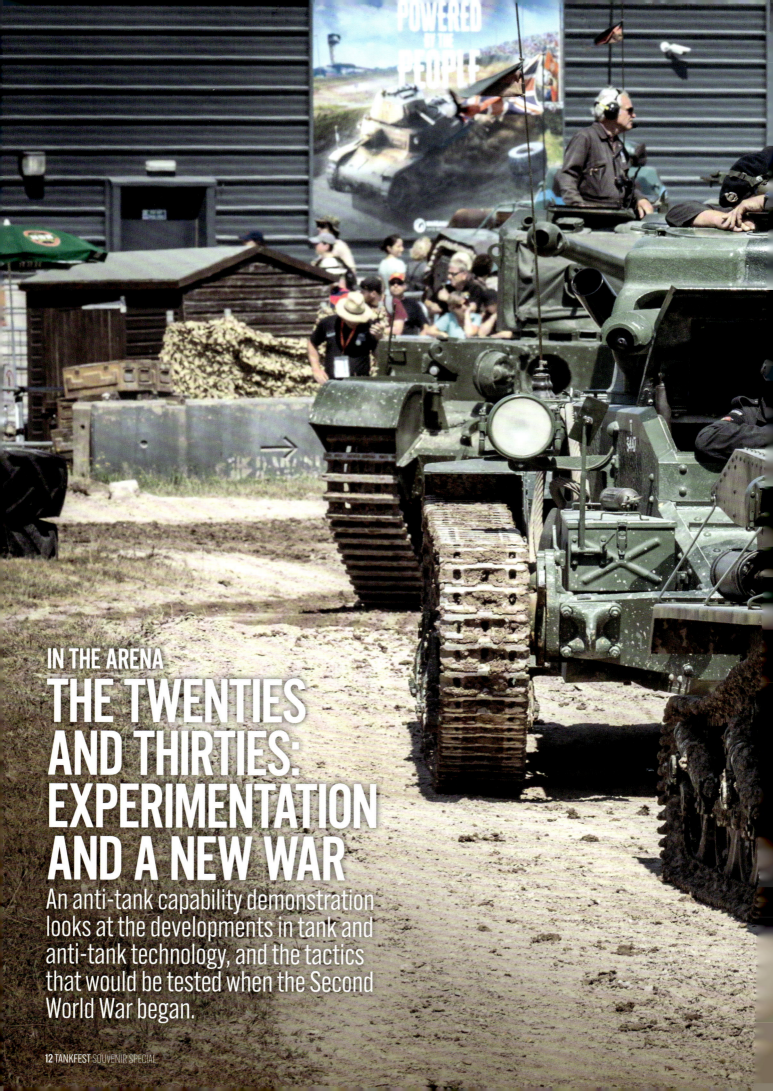

IN THE ARENA
THE TWENTIES AND THIRTIES: EXPERIMENTATION AND A NEW WAR

An anti-tank capability demonstration looks at the developments in tank and anti-tank technology, and the tactics that would be tested when the Second World War began.

The Tank Museum's Light Tank Mark IV leads the Matilda I around the arena at a recent TANKFEST.

The Tank Museum's Tank, Infantry Mark I Matilda (A11) was recovered from the Army's Otterburn Ranges where it had been used as a target. It was later restored by Bob Grundy.

'Many of the bogie wheels and the suspension for the Matilda I came from a Soviet T-26 wreck in Norway.'

LIGHT TANK MARK IV AND MATILDA I

Entering service with the British Army in 1935, only about 38 examples of the Light Mark IV were made and it was the last Light Tank with just a two-man crew. It was mainly used for training, but a few ended up in France in 1940 with the BEF and were captured by the Germans. This particular vehicle is a rare survivor. David Willey comments: 'The museum's Light Mark IV had a restoration project started a couple of decades ago, but that didn't get very far, so in 2017 it was decided to send it to a private conservator, Armoured Engineering Ltd, in Kent, who returned in to running order.'

The Tank Museum's Matilda I was built in March 1940 and restored to running condition in the 1980s. It is displayed in the markings of the 4th Royal Tank Regiment (4 RTR), at the time of the Battle of France in May 1940. The 'Chinese eye' painted on the turret is a tradition dating back to the First World War and relates to Mr Eu Tong Sen, an ethnic Chinese member of the Federal Council of the Malay States, who paid for a new tank to be constructed by William Foster and Co of Lincoln. In keeping with their traditional use on Chinese ships, he asked that the tank have eyes painted on it.

On exercise, commanders of Light Tank Mark IVs often chose to sit on top of their turrets with their legs dangling down inside. They simply reached through the hatch to fire the machine-gun without sighting it properly.

During the Battle of France in May 1940, crowds of refugees choked the cambered and cobbled roads. These roads played havoc with the Matilda I's flimsy gear linkage.

There was simply too much for two men to do operating a light tank in action, a point that was well-made by two Royal Tank Corps officers when they dubbed it the 'Two-and-a-Half-Man-Light-Tank'.

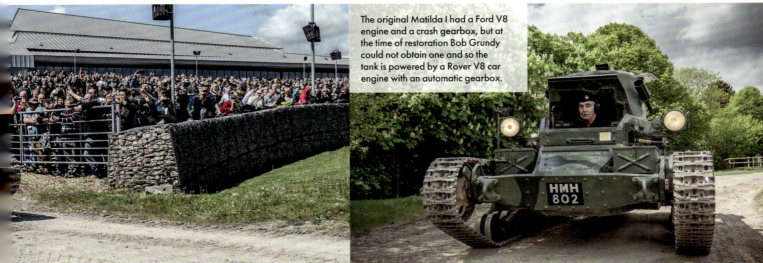

The original Matilda I had a Ford V8 engine and a crash gearbox, but at the time of restoration Bob Grundy could not obtain one and so the tank is powered by a Rover V8 car engine with an automatic gearbox.

The Spanish Civil War veteran Panzer I Ausf B in Madrid's El Goloso museum was used as a data source to enable a faithful replica to be built.

All parts of the tank, including castings, are made from steel. Here, the hull, superstructure and turret can be seen under construction.

REPLICA STORY

BLITZKRIEG PANZER

A full-size running replica of a German Panzer I Ausf B light tank is set to make its UK debuts at Tiger Day and TANKFEST 2023. **Jonathan Falconer** spoke to its creator, **Jose Martine**z, to find out more about his unique 'Panzer I Project'.

Jose Martinez's meticulously scratch-built Panzer I Ausf B replica is paraded in the Kuwait Arena at Tiger Day in April 2023.

Jose Martinez is the driving force behind a full-size running replica of a Panzer I light tank that was the main vehicle used by the German tank force up to the beginning of the Second World War.

Jose grew up in the Spanish port city of Cádiz where the Army and Navy are very much in evidence. With his own family links to the armed forces it was perhaps inevitable that he would develop a passion for military collecting. 'It's a hobby that has grown over the years and I've got to know many people from this little group of enthusiasts who have shown me a whole host of ever more interesting pieces. A few years ago, I was introduced to the world of tanks and military vehicles, which I fell in love with straight away for their design and technical attributes,' he says.

Access to rare Panzer I's

Although Spain was not an active participant in the Second World War, in 1939 it found it had inherited a lot of military equipment and vehicles from the Spanish Civil War of 1936–39, which had been used as a testing ground for weapons by Nazi Germany, Fascist Italy and Soviet Russia, who supported the Nationalist and Republican factions. 'This has meant we have a great deal

TANKFEST *Souvenir Special* **19**

For authenticity, Jose and his team closely followed original German specifications when it came to the gauge of steel they used.

The turret and running gear were the most difficult parts to manufacture due to their complexity. Manufacturer's marks were incorporated into the track castings as an example of the attention to detail.

Ready for the Mercedes-Benz engine to be installed. The running gear is an authentic reproduction of the original. The wheels are aluminium.

Primer is applied to the superstructure prior to application of the camouflage paint scheme.

of German, Italian, Russian and some French early stuff. In fact, in Spain we have two original Panzer Is in Madrid. There are very few museums worldwide that have this tank and it seemed like a good idea to build a replica because we could readily access the originals,' explains Jose. 'It's also a small tank and relatively straightforward to replicate without having to call on heavy engineering resources.'

The Museo de Medios Acorazados de El Goloso in Madrid has two Panzer Is in their collection, a PzKpfw I Ausf A and Ausf B, which have been an invaluable resource for Jose. 'They helped a lot, allowing me to access data, make videos and take measurements of the original tanks. This was a great help in understanding the design to enable me to reproduce parts as faithfully as possible,' he says.

'The Tank Museum at Bovington helped me enormously, too, with the Commander's Panzer I (Befehlspanzer), providing me with information, measurements and photographs,' he adds.

Not one, but two

Jose decided to build replicas of two different versions in parallel – the Ausf B and Befehlspanzer – because there were economies of scale to be gained from doing so, and in his words, 'this is a project that you only do once in a lifetime'.

Focussing on the Ausf B, how long did it take Jose to build the tank? 'Around five years – and many sleepless nights,' he jokes. 'I paid for it all myself and I had to sell some of my collection, including several artillery pieces, to fund the work. Yes, sometimes I regret having to do this, but the end result has been worth it,' he reflects.

Scratch-building a replica

Building a tank from scratch comes with its own challenges, as Jose explains. 'The main one was the creation of cast components and their machining. Rolling has been the most complex and expensive part of a project like this, and it's especially important if you want to preserve the originality of the design. In addition, everything is made from steel, which presents its own difficulties of manufacture,' he points out.

Externally, the tank is a faithful replica of its 80-year-old subject, the Panzer I Ausf B, but you'll have to be an expert and look very closely to notice what few concessions have been made to modernity by Jose to facilitate its construction. The interior, of course, is modern as is the 150hp 6-cylinder inline Mercedes-Benz petrol engine, with automatic transmission to aid manoeuvrability.

Help from friends and enthusiasts

Jose has been fortunate in having the support of a number of good friends and fellow enthusiasts in building the Panzer I. 'My close friend Miguel González is someone else who shares my passion for military vehicles. I've also had tremendous logistical and professional help from Jesús García. They'll both be coming with me to Bovington for TANKFEST,' he reveals. There are many others around the world who have also assisted Jose in this adventure. 'Without the help of my friend Christoph Gebhardt in Poland (toysforboys4) and his great team, our tank would never have been motorised, giving it the power to move,' he acknowledges.

Future projects
Not one to rest on his laurels, Jose has other projects in the pipeline. 'We are working on new restorations related to vehicles from the Spanish Civil War, such as a Soviet T-26 light tank and Russian and Italian trucks. We are also working with M4 Shermans and M5 half-tracks – and we look forward to showing you the results soon!' he exclaims.

You can follow Jose Martinez and his Panzer I Project on Facebook at www.facebook.com/DerErstePanzer

Immaculate in a paint scheme that was used between the end of the Civil War and the beginning of the Second World War, the Panzer I wears emblems of the Spanish Legion and the Panzer-Gruppe Drohne. The black cross on the turret top was to aid identification from the air.

'Building a tank from scratch comes with its own challenges. The main one was the creation of cast components and their machining.'

ANTI-TANK WEAPONS

PIAT
THE PANZER KILLER

SPECIFICATION
Weight 34½lb (15.5kg)
Length 39in (0.99m)
Calibre 83mm (3.3in)
Muzzle velocity 260ft (80m)/sec
Effective firing range 345ft (105m)
Maximum firing range 1,050ft (320m)
Sights Aperture sight
Filling Shaped charge
Filing weight 2½lb (1.1kg)
Detonation mechanism Impact

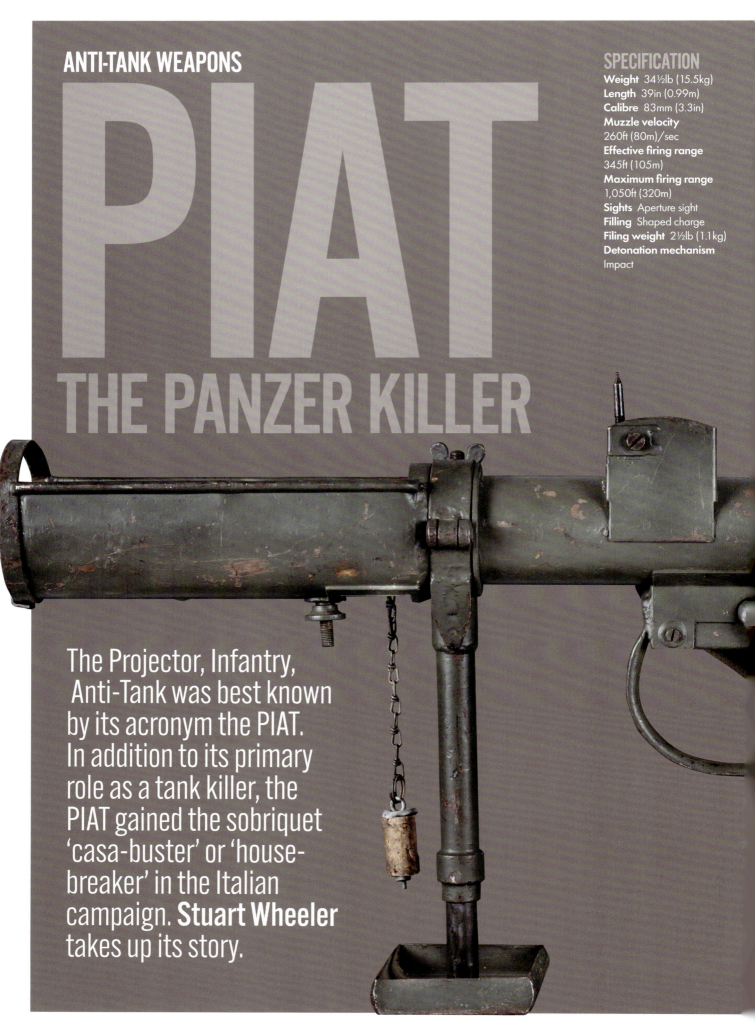

The Projector, Infantry, Anti-Tank was best known by its acronym the PIAT. In addition to its primary role as a tank killer, the PIAT gained the sobriquet 'casa-buster' or 'house-breaker' in the Italian campaign. **Stuart Wheeler** takes up its story.

The need to spread the word about the effectiveness of the newly introduced PIAT anti-tank weapon in the Second World War saw successful actions being highlighted and communicated to troops. In one such encounter in December 1943, Canadian Sergeant Jean Paul Joseph Rousseau of the Royal 22e Régiment got to within 105ft (32m) of a Panzer IV in Italy, hitting the turret and causing a secondary ammunition explosion that destroyed the tank and its crew. He had been supported with covering fire from his platoon.

First Canadian Division highlighted Rousseau's success, for which he would later receive the Military Medal, in a Training Memorandum, stating that this action: 'demonstrated clearly that enemy tanks can be dealt with effectively by infantry men who have confidence in their weapons and the ability to use them'. This use of memoranda to advertise successful engagements was important, emphasising to troops that the PIAT if handled properly was a tank-killing weapon, and was similar to the training film that had been used to reinforce the idea that the Boys anti-tank Rifle was still a capable weapon.

Ultimately, six Victoria Crosses would be awarded to Allied soldiers using a PIAT in the Second World War.

The Baby Bombard

Britain started the war with the Boys Anti-tank Rifle and a grenade that could be fired from a cup container on a rifle as their anti-tank weapons for the common infantryman. Both proved ineffective in service so new designs were sought.

Lieutenant Colonel Latham Valentine Stewart Blacker had a *Boys Own* career, serving on the North West Frontier in the RFC in the First World War, and carrying out such daring exploits as flying over Mount Everest. He set himself up as a weapons designer and helped create a spigot weapon called the Blacker Bombard that some units of the Home Guard were issued with in 1940. Another of his designs – the Baby Bombard – was further developed by Major Millis Jefferis who worked at a unit called MD1 making weapons for a range of roles, but primarily for undercover work.

The Tank Museum's Projector, Infantry, Anti-Tank (PIAT) with bomb. The simple design of the PIAT belied its potency in use.

TANKFEST SOUVENIR SPECIAL 23

HM King George VI is treated to a demonstration of the Blacker Bombard.

BOMB, HE/AT, INFANTRY PROJECTOR, AT MARK 1

1. Plug, fuse hole
2. Spring
3. Fuse holder
4. Detonator No 66 Mk 2
5. Fore body
6. Cordtex
7. Union ring
8. Cone, steel
9. Explosive 808
10. Central tube guide bush
11. Detonator No 66 Mk 1
12. GE pellet
13. Felt disc
14. Cartridge
15. Tail tube
16. Inner tube
17. Tail unit
18. Dust excluder
19. Loading clip

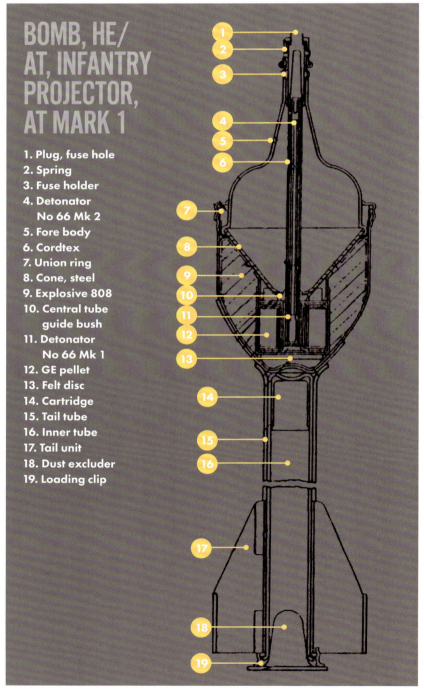

Using hollow charge ammunition, Jefferis rebuilt the Baby Bombard and had it test-fired at Bisley. The first firer was injured from metal flying back from the target, leading Jefferis to take over the demonstration. Although the weapon had a number of faults, it was put into production in August 1942 as the PIAT Mark 1 bomb.

A further demonstration in November 1942 confirmed the PIAT's capabilities, with three PIATs registering five hits in 20 seconds on a moving Churchill. The PIAT was now ready to be introduced to the Panzer and it was first used in Tunisia in 1943. Orders followed for 100,000 PIATs, 10 million live rounds as well as numerous practice rounds. ICI started to gear up to manufacture 10,000 PIATs, with 50 rounds of ammunition each from January 1943 and by the Normandy campaign the following year, each platoon of infantry would have a PIAT with a two-man team – a firer and a loader.

PIAT – Projector, Infantry, Anti-Tank

In terms of size, the PIAT is not a particularly large weapon, measuring 39in, or just under a metre long. Even though it had not achieved its target weight of 28lb, it could still be carried by one man. It now weighed in at 34½lb (15.5kg) and it would have been a hefty metal lump to carry around for any length of time – although if you'd transported the Blacker Bombard you would have considered it to be lightweight in comparison.

Taking the PIAT Mark 4 bomb as an example, it would have been stored in its container and was usually carried in sets of three. Each bomb would have its No 426 graze fuse attached to the tail ready for the loader to arm later. The retaining clip was located at the end of the tube and a drum tail fin fitted to stabilise the projectile in flight. A propellant cartridge, when ignited, propelled the bomb towards the target, at 260ft (80m)/sec. The Mark 4 bomb differed from the Mark 3 due to the insertion of two mild steel discs just in front of the cartridge. This modification was added because it had been found that when the warhead detonated on the target, it flung fragments back through the tail tube at 3,000ft

Instructors demonstrate how to fire a Boys anti-tank rifle.

Lieutenant Colonel Latham Valentine Stewart Blacker.

Above: The Grenade, Rifle No 68 Anti-Tank was one of the first operational weapons to adopt the shaped charge principle, but it proved little better than the Boys anti-tank rifle.

Main picture: A soldier from 32nd Guards Brigade sets up his PIAT near St Martin-des-Besaces in Normandy on 1 August 1944. The village and its environs were the scene of bitter fighting during Operation Bluecoat.

(914m)/sec towards the operator causing injuries. The main body of the Mark 4 projectile featured a 50/50 explosive mix of RDX and TNT, with the steel liner separating the shaped charge cavity here. A Cordtex detonator was centrally located in the body, and linked the explosive to the graze fuse. This No 426 fuse had the safety feature of arming during flight rather than when being handled.

Hard to handle

Moreover, the PIAT remained difficult for all users when in action as the initial cocking operation invariably required the operator to attempt to cock the spring lying on their back. There are soldiers' accounts of the PIAT that give an impression of their wariness of the 200lb/sq in mainspring and its ability to cause damage to the operator, whether cocking or firing.

First, they would need to position their feet either side of the butt, with the bomb support over one shoulder. Then, with one hand grasping the trigger guard underneath, and the other hand any part which gave good leverage, the operator would sit up or bend their knees, depending on cover, and pull the outer casing away from the shoulder-piece and turn it anti-clockwise as far as it would go. The instruction continued that 'pushing with your feet and pulling with the hands on the outer casing' was necessary until you 'heard a click'. As you can imagine, this was not an easy operation to achieve with an enemy in close-proximity and hence the exhortation to always keep your PIAT unloaded but cocked at all times.

Two-man team

While the PIAT could be operated by one person, it was officially seen as a two-man weapon – one, to fire, the second to load. Before the bomb could be fired the fuse had to be inserted. To load, number two first

> 'Pushing with your feet and pulling with the hands on the outer casing was necessary until you heard a click.'

IMPHAL – LAMA VC

In Burma, 19-year-old Rifleman Ganju Lama, 1st Battalion, 7th Gurkha Rifles, engaged a platoon of Japanese tanks in village fighting around Imphal in June 1944. Lama's VC citation revealed that under heavy enemy fire he had crawled within 30yds of the tanks, this despite suffering a broken wrist and other wounds, to knock out two Type 97 Chi Ha tanks, ultimately stalling the Japanese attack and forcing them to retreat.

'In an action near Medjez el Bab, Tunisia, Sergeant Oscroft saw his PIAT round glance off a Tiger I – The Tank Museum's famous Tiger 131.'

removed the dust plug from the bomb tail, removing the muzzle plug followed by the thimble. He inserted the fuse and then replaced the thimble. The bomb was then placed nose first, with fins to the rear, in the bomb support so that the guide ring was engaged between the guide plates to prevent misfires and to secure the bomb so it did not fall out if depressing the PIAT for firing. This process would take approximately 2–3 secs. He would then prepare a second bomb.

Sighting
Meanwhile, number one raised the rear and front sights, and adjusted the monopod to line the sights up. The rules for aiming were: 'Against head-on and retiring tanks: keep the foresight in the centre of the aperture and aim at the centre of the tank. Against crossing tanks... aim one length in front of the tank from the centre. The swing of the projector must not be checked at the moment of firing – that is keep tracking and fire.' Advice was given about judging the lead necessary for a tank and increasing elevation at longer ranges.

Fire!
To fire, the number one raised the shoulder piece into the shoulder, pushed the safety catch forward and used his left hand on the gaiter to steady the weapon. The right thumb would go behind the grip and two fingers placed on the trigger. Once the trigger was pressed there was an appreciable delay before the bomb fired. The recoil was described as being a 'steady thrust' – the spring helping to reduce the recoil – but it was important to maintain correct hold and aim during delay or the target might be missed.

What would then happen is that, when the number one pulled the trigger, the spigot would be released and propelled by the tension of the mainspring forward down the full length of the guide tube into the base of the bomb's tail tube. This whole process took one-tenth of a second. Then the firing pin located at the end of the spigot would ignite the propellant cartridge inside the tail which, in turn, would form a gas seal at the top of the tail tube and create the propellant gases, which exited the bomb tail tube and pushed against the spigot head. The pressure of the spigot head, and propellant gases, pushed the bomb forward, dropping the loading clip, and projecting the bomb out of the PIAT at 262ft (80m)/sec, while simultaneously exerting rearward pressure against the spigot, pushing the spring, and sleeve bolt backwards, until they were held in place by the trigger mechanism, which re-cocked the weapon ready for the next bomb. This velocity was almost identical to the M1 Bazooka, but of course the bazooka used an electric current to ignite its rocket, rather than a spigot-initiated firing pin. Also, the PIAT bomb was launched at the end of the weapon, as opposed to the bazooka, which was launched at the rear, and used the whole tube to burn its rocket propellant, and in the process, created a back-blast. This lack of back-blast was one of the benefits of the PIAT's launching mechanism as it allowed it to be fired from enclosed spaces without giving away the operator's position to the enemy.

Panzer killer
In terms of combat use, the PIAT made its debut with infantry units fighting around Medjez el Bab, Tunisia, in March 1943. In an action at Point 174, the following month, a Sergeant Oscroft of 2nd Battalion, The Sherwood Foresters, would see his PIAT round glance off a Tiger I – The Tank Museum's famous Tiger 131.

By September 1943, and the Allied invasion of the Italian mainland, it started to become clear that the PIAT was not only deadly against armour but it also offered the infantry units, those who been issued with it, the ability to nullify pillboxes, and to assist in street fighting, where it would gain the sobriquet 'casa-buster' or 'house-breaker', in its designed secondary role.

The PIAT was also put to good use in Normandy, providing D-Day airborne/air-landing elements with the means to at least defend themselves from German armour counterattacks, as long as their weapons survived the

A PIAT team in the Netherlands during the late summer/autumn of 1944. Note the bomb support tray at the front of the weapon, the raised rear sight and the shoulder piece pushed firmly into the number one's right shoulder.

British soldiers with a PIAT crouch in a snowy roadside ditch while a Churchill Crocodile rumbles past. North West Europe, winter 1944/45.

landing – the 2nd Battalion Ox & Bucks found that all bar one of D Company's PIATs had been damaged in the glider landings around the Orne and Caen Canal. Probably the most famous PIAT actions of all were at Arnhem in September 1944 during Operation Market Garden, a battle subsequently immortalised by that staple of many a Sunday afternoon's television viewing, *A Bridge Too Far*, in which Anthony Hopkins, as Lieutenant Colonel Johnny Frost, cries 'Bring up the PIAT!' as enemy armour crosses the bridge. Apart from a few 6pdr anti-tank guns at their disposal, British First Airborne Corps relied on the PIAT at the platoon level to provide their main anti-tank weapon support.

Frost and his men's gallant fight at the northern end of the bridge halted Gräbner's 9th SS Recce battalion's assault in its tracks leaving 20 burning AFVs smouldering. It was only when the PIATs had depleted their ammunition that German armour was safely able to press forward.

PIATs saw action throughout North West Europe and thousands were supplied to the Soviet Union with little evidence of them being used in action. PIATs were issued to SOE operatives and used by resistance forces, such as the Polish Home Army receiving 250 during the Warsaw Uprising.

The PIAT was also used in Burma and the Pacific mainly against bunkers and other targets of opportunity due to the lack of Japanese tanks as the war progressed. However, when Japanese tanks were in action, and PIATs were available, heroism was the same as it was in Europe. However, by the time of the Korean War in 1950 the PIAT was largely obsolete.

The official War Office small arms training pamphlet for the PIAT, dated 1943.

ARNHEM – CAIN VC

Among the heroism at Arnhem, Major Robert Cain, 2nd Battalion, The South Staffordshire Regiment's actions on 20 September at Oosterbeek stand out. Using the PIAT in a mortar role, Major Cain used its elevation to drop bombs onto a self-propelled AFV on the other side of a house. Cain was subsequently wounded and lost his number two to artillery fire. He was further wounded in the face while engaging to two more tanks, when a second PIAT bomb detonated prematurely in his face as it left the launcher. Not being deterred, Cain picked up another PIAT and started to stalk more German tanks that were advancing towards them. He hit the first tank and was wounded for a third time, but carried on firing until the disabled tank was knocked out by a 75mm pack howitzer.

He continued his one-man Panzer-wrecking onslaught the following day, engaging three more tanks, again with little regard for his personal safety, only swapping to a 2in mortar when the PIAT had run out of ammunition. Major Cain was the only one of five VC recipients at Arnhem to survive.

Far left: Matilda II *The Princess Royal*.
This picture: M5A1 *Astoria* leads M3A1 *Clementine*,
M4A1 *Havoc*, M4A2 *Fury* and M4A2 *Lucy Sue*.

IN THE ARENA
WORLD WAR TWO: LESSONS FROM THE DESERT WAR

28 TANKFEST SOUVENIR SPECIAL

This Churchill III is in the long-term care of The Tank Museum but is owned by The Churchill Trust — a registered charity with common objectives.

Battles across North Africa between the Allied and Axis armies saw a race between increasingly powerful anti-tank guns and the need for thicker armour.

The Panzer III was conceived in 1934 as the principle combat tank of the Panzer divisions. The Tank Museum's Panzer III is believed to have been captured south of El Alamein at the Battle of Alam Halfa in August/September 1942.

TANKFEST SOUVENIR SPECIAL 29

'More than 22,700 M3 Stuarts of all variants were produced in the US between 1941 and 1944, of which 4,621 were the M3A1.'

Left: Churchill III, T31831, with 75mm gun; centre: Matilda II *The Princess Royal*; right: M3A1 *Clementine* with M4A2 *Fury*.

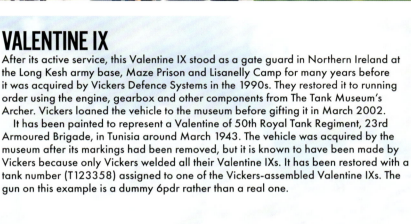

Left: Tiger Day 2023. Above: The Tank Museum's Panzer III is an early production Ausf L and is modified for tropical use.

VALENTINE IX

After its active service, this Valentine IX stood as a gate guard in Northern Ireland at the Long Kesh army base, Maze Prison and Lisanelly Camp for many years before it was acquired by Vickers Defence Systems in the 1990s. They restored it to running order using the engine, gearbox and other components from The Tank Museum's Archer. Vickers loaned the vehicle to the museum before gifting it in March 2002.

It has been painted to represent a Valentine of 50th Royal Tank Regiment, 23rd Armoured Brigade, in Tunisia around March 1943. The vehicle was acquired by the museum after its markings had been removed, but it is known to have been made by Vickers because only Vickers welded all their Valentine IXs. It has been restored with a tank number (T123358) assigned to one of the Vickers-assembled Valentine IXs. The gun on this example is a dummy 6pdr rather than a real one.

M3A1 *Clementine* is owned by the Bannister Collection and was one of 350 Stuarts that saw Brazilian Army service. In October 2008, with 15 others, it was imported from Brazil by RR Motor Services. It now represents a British 'Honey' Stuart from the North Africa campaign.

ANTI-TANK WEAPONS
BAZOOKA AND THE SHAPED CHARGE

Stuart Wheeler describes how the arrival of the shaped charge launcher and specifically the United States Army's development of the bazooka in the Second World War was a watershed moment in anti-tank warfare.

For the US, infantry anti-tank weapons, like most other nations, had not been given a high priority during the inter-war period and the initial focus for the US Army was on automatic weapons like the M2 .50-cal machine-gun, introduced into service in 1933, for their anti-tank capability. It was quickly realised that larger calibre rounds in the form of .6-calibre and later .9-calibre anti-tank rifles would be more effective in this dedicated role, and the purchase of a couple of the 20mm Solothurn rifles in 1939 showed the way that US military thinking was heading.

However, the weight and manoeuvrability of these anti-tank rifles became an issue and the US entered the Second World War without its own manufactured anti-tank rifle, although some Ranger units used the Boys. Simultaneously, other solutions had started to be explored and the bazooka's origin really comes down to the evolution, and marrying, of two distinct developments: the shaped charge warhead and solid rocket propulsion.

Experiments with explosives

The development of what we know as the shaped charge concept is first referenced in the late 18th century with the use of cavity explosives for mining purposes, but it was nearly a century before the first documented experiments on the hollow charge process began in the mid-1880s. During this period, a German, Max von Foerster, started to experiment with compressed nitrocellulose. He was closely followed by another German, Gustav Bloem, who patented the invention of a hemispherical cavity that concentrated and increased the effect of an explosion in an axial direction.

Several years later in 1888, while working for the US Navy on underwater explosive devices, Charles Munroe discovered that a cavity, if surrounded by sticks of dynamite, would concentrate the explosive charge in a focused direction. What became known in the UK and US as the Munroe Effect demonstrated that the hollow charge concept could penetrate steel.

The shaped charge is perfected

However, we have to wait until the experiments of yet another German, Egon Neumann, during the Great War to identify and improve the concept. It was Neumann, who discovered the significance of lining the cavity of the

PRODUCTION
The success of the bazooka as an anti-tank weapon can be seen by the production numbers. 2.36in Bazooka M1 to M18 – approx 476,728 made by the war's end. Over 58 per cent (278, 819) were the M9A1 model. Most bazookas were made by General Electric. Cheney Bigelow Wire Works produced 40,000 M9A1s. The last refinement of the 2.36in launcher model was the M18, which was lighter than the M9A1, but only 500 were produced before the war's end.

Two GI's load a bazooka during training exercises in England in October 1943.

hollow cone of explosive with metal and detonating the charge a short distance away – thus creating the shaped charge concept. In Europe this became known as the von Foerster or Neumann effect.

Further military enhancements to the shaped charge concept had been perfected in the mid-1930s by a Swiss engineer, Henri Mohaupt, who had developed a shaped charge explosive that could penetrate armour. An example of Mohaupt's grenade was supplied to the US Army Ordnance Department and trials followed in December 1940. The result was the creation of the Special Rifle Grenade M9, which was fired from a device attached to the end of a rifle barrel using a specially designed blank cartridge. The M9 entered service with US forces in January 1941, but it was deemed secret so training and usage of it were highly restricted. However,

its main drawback was a lack of armour penetration – 32mm of armour, at a time when armour on tanks was being increased. This meant that until the arrival of an improved hand-held anti-tank weapon, the US infantry would have to rely on the M9A1 rifle grenade for its close-in tank defence.

The M10 Anti-tank Grenade

Initially, work on increasing the armour penetration of the rifle grenade looked promising, with a new design, the M10 high explosive anti-tank grenade. It was accepted in late November 1941 and was capable of defeating 50mm of armour, but it had one drawback: it was deemed too large to be launched from a rifle as it would damage the weapon. Other options were examined, such as a dedicated launcher, but it was Gregory Kissenich, Chief of the Ordnance Patent section, who, in a

SPECIFICATION

M6 Bazooka
Length 55cm (1.8ft)
Diameter 60mm (2.36in)
Weight 1.5kg (3.3lb)
Muzzle velocity 82m (90yds)/sec
Range 275m (300yds)
Propulsion solid-fuelled rocket
Warhead 0.7kg (1.6lb) high explosive Shaped charge

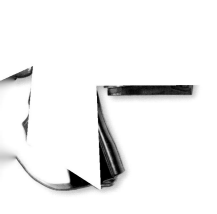

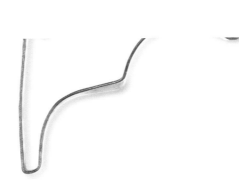

Designed for use by US Airborne units, the M9A1 Bazooka could be broken down into two shorter sections via central coupling lugs.

A training session with an M1 Garand rifle fitted with the M7 grenade-launcher.

South Russia during 1941/42: a German soldier in position with a Solothurn S-18/100 anti-tank rifle. (*Bundesarchiv 1011-189-1250-10*)

serendipitous moment, discovered that new developments in rocket propulsion could provide the solution to the M10 grenade's launching problems.

By August 1941, Kissenich had passed this information to Colonel Wiley Moore, Chief of the Small Arms Division, at Indian Head. He invited Major Skinner and Lieutenant Edward Uhl, who were employed on US Army rocket projects to join him. Together they began to experiment with the M10 grenade and the solid-propellant rocket motors they had been working on. Later, they were joined by a Dr Hickman who was also researching rocket propellant. It is the next two stages that become key to the creation of the bazooka concept: the propellant and the launcher.

The bazooka is born

Initially, spigot mortars, were trialled in an attempt to identify a suitable launcher but this did not produce the required accuracy level. However, it was discovered that if the formulation of the propellant itself was changed, so it had a faster burn time, then the projectile could be launched from a long tube, allowing the rocket motor to burn out before exiting, increasing its accuracy and helping to reduce any propellant scorching to the operator.

Skinner and Uhl progressed developments by creating a working model using a scrap section of 5ft-long metal tube, adding wooden hand grips, a shoulder stock, and rigging up an electrical trigger system using a battery. Uhl demonstrated this device to the assembled delegates at Aberdeen Proving Ground in May 1942, to show that the launcher could hit a moving M3 medium tank, while other spigot-based weapons were unable to achieve this. Apparently, Lieutenant General McNair, Commander of Army Ground Forces, liked what he saw and asked to fire the weapon himself. This led General Barnes, Chief of the Ordnance Technical Staff, who also fired a rocket, to later comment that the launcher resembled the bazooka musical instrument, invented and played by radio and musical comedian Bob Burns.

Bob Burns, radio and musical comedian, with his bazooka instrument, which bears a striking similarity to the bazooka launcher.

The 2.36in Anti-Tank Rocket Launcher M1.

'The T1 was officially designated as the 2.36in M1 anti-tank rocket launcher and M6 HEAT rocket – the age of the bazooka had arrived.'

Contracts are placed

Further demonstrations confirmed the bazooka's success and on 20 May 1942, General Electric's plant at Bridgeport, Connecticut, was awarded the contract for the manufacture of 5,000 of the newly-named T1 launchers, codenamed 'Whip', with the E.G Budd Company, Philadelphia, given the contract to produce 25,000 rockets. After reputedly working through 14 different launcher designs and various improvements to the T1 rockets, General Electric's engineer, James L. Powers, had turned Uhl's crude working design into one that could be mass-produced. A few weeks later, on 24 June 1942, the T1 was officially type-classified as the 2.36in M1 anti-tank rocket launcher and M6 HEAT rocket. The age of the bazooka had arrived.

Bazooka in action

In terms of combat use, the bazooka made its debut for the US Army during the Torch landings in North Africa in early November 1942, with a Renault FT appearing to be the first recorded vehicle casualty. Prior to this, British and Soviet forces had been the first to receive bazookas, but the British stored their launcher allocation in the belief that the bazooka was not suitable for desert fighting, deciding it was difficult to conceal. The Red Army also appears to have had its concerns regarding the bazooka such as concealment, back-blast, and its less effective performance in colder temperatures, and therefore favoured sticking with its anti-tank rifle.

Initial success with the bazooka appears to have been patchy in Tunisia, in the main due to a lack of specific training, and the decision not to have dedicated crews.

SHAPED CHARGE LAUNCH DISTANCE IS CRUCIAL

In basic terms, the whole shaped charge process is designed to direct and concentrate energy in the axial direction creating a deep cavity or penetration, but it requires a specific stand-off distance to allow the jet to form properly. Too near, and the jet won't have time to form; too far away, and the jet will disperse its energy. This means that the initiating distance for the optimum deployment of shaped charge weapons, regardless of the firing or placement method, is crucial to its destructive effectiveness. Armour penetration from Second Word War shaped charges is around two to three times their diameter. Large diameter warheads, different shaped cones and liner materials all had an impact on the effectiveness of the warhead's armour penetration.

With smoke from destroyed German armour filling the sky, American troops – one carrying a bazooka – move on toward Fontainebleau en route to Paris on 23 August 1944.

By the time the landings in Sicily and Salerno had taken place the following year the bazooka's reputation as an effective defensive weapon had been made.

Initially, bazookas were allotted three to a Rifle Company, but this changed in February 1944 with the addition of five more, bringing the total to eight in each Rifle Company and dedicated crews allocated. An M6 canvas bag held three rockets each and three bags were carried per bazooka.

Normandy and the Ardennes

In Normandy in 1944, and especially with its employment in the sunken lanes of the Bocage country, the bazooka was seen as much more capable than the 57mm anti-tank gun (which was viewed as unwieldly). It was also used in an offensive role against German strongpoints, such as pillboxes and bunkers, giving the infantry another direct-fire weapon.

The bazooka proved valuable to infantry and airborne units in the Ardennes, with nine times as many rockets

WARHEAD

The bazooka warhead is manufactured from thin pressed sheet steel with the explosive cone spaced cavity sitting inside a 2mm copper liner. Liner thickness, shape and material choice was crucial: the change from a steel to a copper liner increased penetration by around 30°, allowing up to 5in (or 127mm) of armour to be penetrated. As the warhead hits the target, the fuse located above it is immediately initiated by the impact travelling through the walls, detonating the explosive. This in turn creates a high-pressure shockwave, which collapses the copper liner into a hypersonic jet. The tip of the jet is travelling much faster (10km/s) in comparison to the base (2km/s) as it has more time to form. The metal liner essentially resembles a hydrodynamic fluid, rather than a solid, and heats up to more than 800° Celsius during the process. Metal fragments from the projectile could also hit the crew behind the penetrated armour as well as igniting ammunition and fuel.

The M6A1 HEAT rocket had a pointed nose compared to the later round-shaped nose of the M6A3.

being fired than in June 1944. However, the thicker sloped armour on the Panther and King Tiger started to show the 2.36in bazooka's limitations, with track and flanking shots being the only real options of obtaining a hit. Also, the cold winter weather was reported as having an adverse effect on the batteries of the earlier models. They were duly allotted to the Pacific theatre, but there was less requirement for them due to the lack of a Japanese armour threat.

An effective anti-tank weapon

The invention of the bazooka gave the US foot soldier a stand-off weapon with an effective anti-tank capability for the first time. It was relatively easy to learn how to operate, it was transportable and able to be concealed. Its arrival on the battlefield provided the infantry with a direct-fire weapon to be used against massed tank attacks – 4.5 per cent of German tank losses were attributed to the bazooka, and in offensive roles against strongpoints.

Of course, there were drawbacks. The bazooka's limited calibre meant it was outdated by the end of 1944 against tanks using sloped armour, and the need to expose the operator to fire the weapons mean that it was vulnerable to infantry and artillery fire, not to mention the problems of back-blast. But even when 'hits' did not penetrate thicker armour, or it failed to ignite, the bazooka offered the infantry a tangible upgrade on the anti-tank rifle and the anti-tank grenade during 1943 and 1944 – and one they were grateful to have.

Refining the design

The last refinement of the 2.36in launcher model was the M18, which was lighter than the M9A1, but only 500 were produced before the war's end. The key feature of the M18 was the reduction in weight it offered over the M9A1 – 5.57lb, which was due to its aluminium construction. Other developments saw trials in 1943 of 3.25in launchers, the T16 and T24, aimed at providing an increase in penetration, but these designs were not pursued.

Increases in armour protection, especially the use of sloped armour on tanks such as the Panther, led to work on the T74 – a 3.5in aluminium model that could penetrate thicker armour reputedly upwards of 11in (280mm). This model, the M20, would become available in October 1945, but would not see full production and widespread use until the poor performance of the 2.36in bazookas against North Korean T-34-85s in 1950. In contrast, the 'super bazooka' or '3.5' gave infantry the capability of overmatching sloped armour. In addition, different types of rocket were produced including Practice rockets, WP (White Phosphorus) and HC Smoke rounds for target marking and screening. A chemical rocket M26 was developed and filled with cyanogen chloride, but it was never used in action.

Korean War: during their defence of the Pusan perimeter on 18 August 1950, US Marines carrying Super Bazookas file past knocked-out North Korean T-34 tanks.

'The T1 was officially designated as the 2.36in M1 anti-tank rocket launcher and M6 HEAT rocket – the age of the bazooka had arrived.'

A Leathernecks bazooka team of the US 1st Marine Division on Okinawa in 1945 give fire support to a patrol ahead of them.

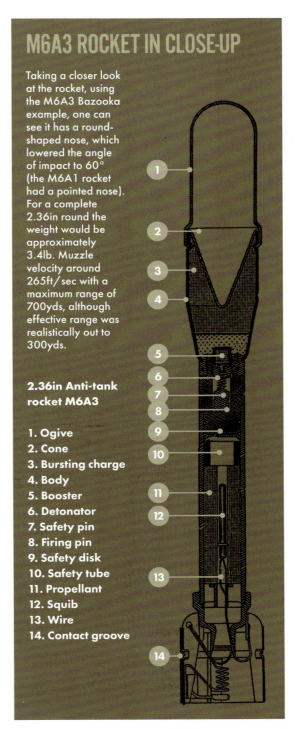

M6A3 ROCKET IN CLOSE-UP

Taking a closer look at the rocket, using the M6A3 Bazooka example, one can see it has a round-shaped nose, which lowered the angle of impact to 60° (the M6A1 rocket had a pointed nose). For a complete 2.36in round the weight would be approximately 3.4lb. Muzzle velocity around 265ft/sec with a maximum range of 700yds, although effective range was realistically out to 300yds.

2.36in Anti-tank rocket M6A3

1. Ogive
2. Cone
3. Bursting charge
4. Body
5. Booster
6. Detonator
7. Safety pin
8. Firing pin
9. Safety disk
10. Safety tube
11. Propellant
12. Squib
13. Wire
14. Contact groove

TANKFEST SOUVENIR SPECIAL 37

A34 Comet I *Cestus* plays to the crowds at Tank Fest 2016. Designed as an upgrade to the Cromwell tank, the Comet entered service in 1945 and conducted occupation duties in Germany. This vehicle is widely regarded as the best tank Britain produced during the Second World War.

Far left: The iconic Soviet T-34/85.

Left: The Infantry Tank Mark III Valentine went through a large number of variants before production ended in 1944.

Right: The M4 Sherman was the most prolific Western tank of the Second World War, playing a crucial role on all fronts, in all theatres, by all Allied armies.

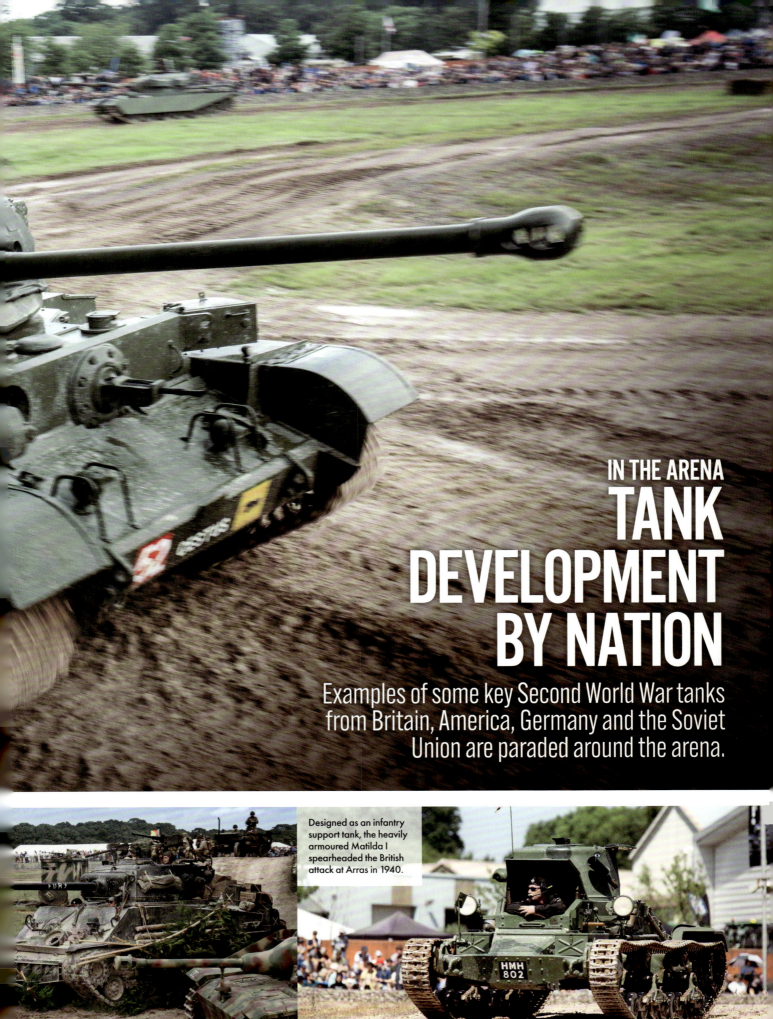

IN THE ARENA
TANK DEVELOPMENT BY NATION

Examples of some key Second World War tanks from Britain, America, Germany and the Soviet Union are paraded around the arena.

Designed as an infantry support tank, the heavily armoured Matilda I spearheaded the British attack at Arras in 1940.

TANKFEST SOUVENIR SPECIAL 39

Q&A

The Tank Museum's Curator, **David Willey**, answers questions about the museum's centenary year, TANKFEST 2023 and the future of the tank as a weapon of war.

Q How important is this centenary year to The Tank Museum?

A Being the world's first and oldest Tank Museum is a distinction we live with and are proud of. For its staff, marking the 100th anniversary is another milestone in the museum's story that is taken in their stride along with the many other activities they're involved with. We were very conscious that, for the public, the 100th anniversary in itself is not necessarily an engaging topic for an exhibition – but it's a great way of reminding people about their own memories of a visit to The Tank Museum. We hope we have brought out some of those memories and an opportunity to share them in our lively new 'Tanks for the Memory' exhibition, which looks at the tank in popular culture. Here, you can see how the tank has appeared in films, art, toys, video games, comics, books and models.

Q Why did you choose anti-tank warfare as the theme for this year's TANKFEST?

A Looking at the news media and its reflections on the war in Ukraine has helped inform our choice of the anti-tank theme. It's ironic that not many months back the tank was being declared redundant. This story of the constant redundancy of the tank as new weapons are developed to defeat armour is one reflected in the museum. Being able to tell this story by looking at those vehicles we display in the arena seems particularly pertinent and will hopefully give a thread to our theme through the chronological displays. The pre-eminence of the tank as the land-based weapon and the constant challenge to this dominance is a tale that has affected why tanks look as they do – and it is, of course, a story that continues.

Q What are the key participants we should look out for this year?

A We always like pointing out guest vehicles like this year's Panzer I or Nashorn, but to be honest as most visitors are new to TANKFEST, just seeing that amount of armour on the move is quite an occasion. Any one of these tanks moving in the public eye would be an 'event' elsewhere, so seeing this number of historic and modern vehicles together is an amazing experience.

Q With the ongoing war in Ukraine, can you explain the relevance of armour on the battlefield after policymakers in recent years have declared the tank obsolete as a weapon of war?

A The war in Ukraine has highlighted how the tank is not only vulnerable to a new range of weapons, but also how it is still hugely important in land warfare. Here we can see that taking and holding ground has a fundamental importance, and tanks are weapons that enable you to do this. A drone or plane has to return to its base and cannot hold ground – if you are a Ukrainian holding ground, your territory is of such importance.

Q How do you see the future of the tank in the light of this?

A There will be – in fact there already is – a reappraisal of how militaries expect to fight future wars. The emphasis is on the need for technologically advanced weapons and defensive aids on vehicles, alongside the reappearance of force size as a determining factor – greater numbers in terms of equipment and soldiers. The expectations that conflicts would be short and sharp has been challenged and the obvious lack of 'puff' in many NATO countries (by this I mean the lack of resources or reserves) is going to need addressing. The need for munitions in quantity – even simple 155mm shells – has been brought to the fore. Hopefully, NATO will have time to react.

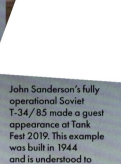

John Sanderson's fully operational Soviet T-34/85 made a guest appearance at Tank Fest 2019. This example was built in 1944 and is understood to have been damaged during the Battle for Prague before proceeding to fight in the Battle for Berlin. The T-34 was the most produced tank ... an improvement on its predecessor, the T-34/76.

BIO

In 1969, six-year-old David Willey made his first visit to The Tank Museum. His Dad tried to concentrate on the exhibits while David spent the day clambering on tanks. He was a frequent visitor to the museum over the years until, in 2000, David became The Tank Museum's Curator (but they don't let him climb on the tanks any more).

Left: Explaining the finer points of the Matilda II's turret to a visitor.

Below left: Valentine IX in the arena at Tiger Day 9.

The Bannister Collection's rare M4A4 Sherman *Belle* at TANKFEST 2022.

'Seeing this number of historic and modern vehicles together is an amazing experience.'

MATILDA II

The Matilda II was dominant in the Western Desert battlefield between the autumn of 1940 and the spring of 1941. It first saw action at the Battle of Arras in 1940 and was the only British tank used throughout the Second World War.

There are two Matilda IIs in The Tank Museum's collection – one running and one a non-runner.

The running example was manufactured on 28 May 1941 by the North British Locomotive Company. It went to the School of Tank Technology at Chertsey and was transferred to The Tank Museum in 1949. In 2016, it underwent a restoration by the Workshop Team, which was completed in May 2018.

Chris van Schaardenburgh, Head of Collections at The Tank Museum, commented: 'The Matilda II tank had been operated by the museum for several years but had developed several mechanical problems, which prevented it from further running. Therefore, there was a feeling of responsibility to repair what had become unserviceable while in our care. The Matilda II is also a very significant British Second World War tank, which the leadership of The Tank Museum felt was needed to be kept as an example in a running condition; there is currently no other running Matilda II in the United Kingdom.'

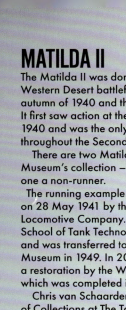
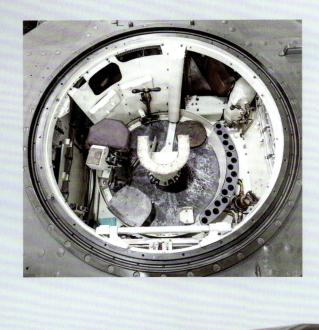

The M24 light tank entered service with the US Army in winter 1944, during the Battle of the Bulge. British Army units that operated the Chaffee included the reconnaissance squadrons of the 7th Armoured Division (the Desert Rats). This vehicle is part of the Bannister Collection.

'Restoring an 80-year-old tank to pristine "as-new" condition is not a job for the faint hearted.'

The Churchill tank was one of the key British tank designs of the Second World War, first seeing action in the Dieppe Raid, in North Africa at El Alamein and in Tunisia, Italy and North West Europe. On long-term loan from the Churchill Trust, this is the only running example of its kind in existence.

Lessons learned from the tank battles in the Western Desert in 1942 led to the development of the last operational cruiser tank, the A34 Comet. The first production Comets reached armoured regiments in September 1944.

TANKFEST SOUVENIR SPECIAL 43

THE GREATEST LIVE SHOW OF HISTORIC MOVING ARMOUR
Inside the complex planning of TANKFEST

INTERVIEW

Every year, over three explosive days in June, more than 20,000 visitors descend on The Tank Museum for TANKFEST – the world's best live displays of historic moving armour, supported by talks, demonstrations and living history. **Jonathan Falconer** met **Rosanna Dean**, Visitor Experience General Manager at The Tank Museum, to discover what it takes to put on such a complex live event.

Planning for the next TANKFEST begins almost as soon as the last TANKFEST visitors have left the site. 'Twenty years ago, the event was biennial and with a mere 4 per cent of the audience we have today,' says Rosanna. 'In 2008, it became an annual event and has grown ever since to welcome over 23,000 people across three days.'

Work on planning and organising TANKFEST continues through the year. 'As a part of our daily job, there are between five and seven of us at the museum who meet almost weekly. Once an overall vision is in place, additional department heads are then invited to meet as and when required to plan their areas in more detail – this could be more members of the events department, catering, front of house, workshops and so on. However, the Events and Workshops teams lead on the administration over this time,' explains Rosanna.

Listening to feedback
As you might expect for such a complex event, there are a number of stages in the planning journey that will bring TANKFEST to the public. 'Our first port of call is to look at both internal and external feedback from the most recent Tankest,' discloses Rosanna. 'The Department Heads responsible for TANKFEST's strategy sit down and discuss key changes and improvements that need to be made from a visitor experience, as well as from budgeting and operational points

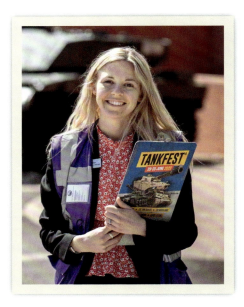

'Twenty years ago, the event was biennial and with a mere 4 per cent of the audience of 23,000 we have today.'

of view, ready for next year,' she says. 'This helps ensure we are delivering the safest, most enjoyable and cost-effective event possible.'

Building on last year's experience
With clear visions of improvement or continuation outlined, the next phase of discussion is strictly curatorial – what is the theme for next year? What vehicle availability is there likely to be for guest appearances, and how will this shape the event? 'Pulling on the conclusions from feedback and curatorial strategy, we then start to really delve into the overall site map, assessing capacity of what can be put where – both curatorially speaking and while working operationally,

too. It's a tough balance to master and something we will genuinely find ourselves striving to improve every year,' she admits.

Suppliers – keeping it local
With site planning in full swing, and June being such a busy month for the events industry in general, it's crucial for Rosanna and her team to lock in suppliers as early as possible – in most cases at least nine months in advance to ensure they have them secured for the following year. 'With this we try to stay as local as possible, not only to support local businesses, but to help with our carbon footprint as well,' she points out. 'We've grown to have such a great network of collaborative relationships over the years and without those TANKFEST wouldn't be the success it is today,' she says proudly.

Traders, exhibitors and living history
Just as the events season is wrapping up for the current year, the events team launch applications for the following. 'Typically speaking, we open for traders, exhibitors and living history in early November, with applications being processed from January,' comments Rosanna. 'This action continues up until and including the event itself and involves some important desk work – processing information, chasing relevant health and safety documentation, contracting, invoicing and building the site map, too,' she points out. 'A few weeks out from the event all arrival information is sent, inductions forms to the site are asked to be returned and the events department are busy making sure they have everything ready to go for trader check-in and set up.'

Spreading the word
With the external contracting now in full motion, the attention of Rosanna and colleagues turns towards operational detailing and curatorial programming both for the main arena and stage. 'It's at this point that we'll start contacting potential speakers, living history groups, vehicle owners and potential sponsors about being involved in the event,' says Rosanna. 'The Marketing Department will already have been promoting TANKFEST for quite some time, but securing and announcing these bookings

BIO

Rosanna Dean is a graduate of Arts University Bournemouth. She is an arts and events professional, joining The Tank Museum in 2018 as Events Manager before becoming Visitor Experience General Manager in 2021.

allow for a drip-feed set of announcements via email, social media, the website and news stories in the months leading up to the event to help entice visitors and encourage more people to attend,' she reveals.

Keeping it safe
While the events team are busily pulling together the programme, they are simultaneously collating their planning information into an Event Management Plan. This document, created in conjunction with the museum's Health and Safety Advisor, is then presented to a Safety Advisory Group at Dorset Council where they check the proposals, processes and make recommendations. 'Our relationship with the local authority, via our Safety Advisory Group, is probably most crucial, because we work with them to ensure we are delivering an operationally safe event,' says Rosanna.

With the event plan, site and general operations plans taking good shape, Rosanna and the Head of Commercial Operations then lead the staffing aspect of the event, allocating roles, booking and planning training, both internally and externally. 'One of the key activities we do each year is a "table-top" exercise,' she says. 'This is where key staff are presented with different emergency scenarios and are required to work through how they would deal with them on the event day. It's not only a great way for our team to get their heads into "events mode", but it also allows them to gain confidence in their role. And it gives the central management team the chance to test and review Event Control operations and emergency plans and make any adjustments prior to the event, if deemed necessary,' discloses Rosanna.

Almost there
Two weeks out from the event, work begins on marking out key pitches and locations ready for them to be built – grandstands, screens, stages, living history pitches and so on. By this time, multiple structures will already have been built (signage, furniture, etc) ready for use, too.

With the museum being on an MOD site, it has of course to be respectful to its landlords regarding any major site decisions. 'We're fortunate that the majority of the event infrastructure is temporary and therefore has minimum impact to the site itself,' explains Rosanna. 'One key additional agreement for us, however, is obtaining further licences for extended car parking in the fields surrounding the museum. Without these fields, having 9,000 people per day on site wouldn't be possible,' she adds.

What's new for TANKFEST 2023?
In recent years, particularly during COVID, the event site has undergone a dramatic review. 'Many of the things we implemented during the pandemic have stayed following positive visitor feedback through our surveys, our stage area being a prime example, which we are pleased to bring back again for 2023,' says Rosanna. 'This year's new addition is TANK TV, which should allow our visitors to have a significantly better viewing experience up-close in the arena, whilst providing additional entertainment, too,' she declares.

A plan comes together
Obtaining the right balance of safe operations, good visitor experience for all tank enthusiast levels, whilst making sure it works as a fundraising event, are the key objectives of the TANKFEST planning team. 'Sometimes these three factors don't work hand-in-hand and it can be challenging to find a good middle ground,' admits Rosanna.

As for the three event days themselves, all museum staff and volunteers work the events and their rota includes approximately 150 per day, with additional support from contractors. On a personal level, a successful TANKFEST is immensely rewarding for Rosanna: 'We're so lucky to have such a diverse workforce, who are willing to do something completely different to their normal job for a day or two and play such a crucial part in our biggest charity fundraiser of the year,' she acknowledges. 'It's hard work, but being one of the central individuals leading the project from start to end, there is nothing more rewarding than seeing the finished result, with the rest of the museum on board to support you.'

TANKFEST offers the world's best live displays of historic moving armour, supported by talks, demonstrations and living history.

TANKFEST SOUVENIR SPECIAL **45**

RESTORATION STORY
NASHORN PHOENIX

It hardly seems possible that this historic Nashorn tank hunter was virtually destroyed in a workshop fire and then brought back to life by a dedicated restoration team at Overloon in the Netherlands. **Craig Moore** looks at the restoration and some of the challenges faced by the team. Pictures by **Robby van Sambeek**.

On 10 March 2019, the result of four years of blood, sweat and tears was destroyed in 30 minutes by a catastrophic fire.

During the invasion of France in 1940 and the Soviet Union in 1941, the German Army encountered heavily armoured enemy tanks that were difficult to knock out. The Panzer III and IV turrets were not large enough to mount the effective high-velocity 8.8cm gun and the Germans needed a quick and cheap stop-gap solution while waiting for the Tiger and Panther tanks to be produced in adequate numbers. Among the many solutions was the Nashorn, a powerful tank destroyer that gained a fearsome reputation.

The vehicle had several long official designations over its design and production run, including this mouthful from September 1944: 8.8cm PaK 43/1 auf Fahrgestell Panzerkampfwagen III und IV Selbstfahrlafette (Sd. Kfz. 164). Even the official abbreviation was long, which is why nicknames became popular among the troops. It was first known as the Hornisse (Hornet) until in late 1943, Hitler ordered the name be changed from a small insect to Nashorn (Rhinoceros) as it sounded 'beefier' and more warlike.

The Nashorn design programme started in 1942 when an 8.8cm PaK 43/1 anti-tank gun was mounted on a specially designed Alkett/Rheinmetall-Borsig lengthened German tank hull called the Geschützwagen III/IV (a vehicle fitted with a gun was called a Geschützwagen, which is translated as a gun vehicle).

Readily available components were used from both the Panzer III and the Panzer IV tank hulls. The Nashorn hull was mostly the same as that of the Panzer IV, but with the width of a Panzer III. This resulted in the final drive, front drive sprocket wheels and steering units plus the Zahnradfabrik SSG 77 transmission gearbox being adopted from the Panzer III as they fitted the hull width better. The features used from the Panzer IV tank were the suspension, idler wheel with track tension adjustment, return rollers, and the Maybach HL 120 TRM engine with its cooling system.

Using existing components enabled a quicker design-to-production timeline. The engine was moved from the rear of the tank chassis to the centre of the vehicle to make room for the gun and the armoured fighting compartment at the back of the vehicle. This is why there are armoured louvred engine air intakes and air exhaust grills in the centre of the vehicle's superstructure sidewalls. It remained in production until March 1945 with 494 produced.

Resurrecting the Rhino

The not-for-profit Nashorn Restoration Project dates to 2015. Project leader, Robby van Sambeek, lives near the Overloon War Museum in the Netherlands, the same museum that runs the annual Militracks event. Robby's day job is as a draughtsman and welder, but in his spare time he has always worked on vehicle and technical construction projects. He is part of a team of volunteers and their families who gave up their spare time to bring this piece of Second World War history back to life.

'In 2015, our group was looking for a restoration project and heard about parts from a Nashorn up for sale,' said Robby. 'It did not include a hull. The parts were found in the Kaliningrad area of Russia, formerly known as Königsberg. A hull was then advertised for sale, which we purchased. It also came from the Kaliningrad area.

'Not much is known about its operational history, but the damage on the superstructure suggests that it was shot at by ground-attack aircraft. The hull had the Fahrgestell serial number 310163. It would have been issued to a schwerer Panzerjäger-Abteilungen (heavy tank hunter battalion) on the Eastern Front where it was knocked out.'

When talking about whether a German tank or self-propelled gun was an early or late model, there are a few things to look out for on the Nashorn. On the early production models, the spare wheel holders were fitted to the front of the superstructure. In the late production vehicles, the spare wheel holders were relocated to below the rear hatches. Robby has mounted the spare wheel holders on their Nashorn at the front of the vehicle, either side of the gun shield.

Early production Nashorns had two headlights and the late production vehicles only had one headlight. The first batch had a large exhaust silencer fitted at the back, underneath the rear hatches. However, crews complained as they repeatedly got burnt getting in and out of the vehicle. The exhaust silencer boxes were removed on the battlefield while late production Nashorns were not fitted with silencers. 'For historical accuracy, we also removed the silencer box,' said Robby.

A major setback

The restoration project suffered a significant setback in 2019 when the vehicle was severely damaged in a fire. 'We had completed work on the engine, suspension system and tracks. The superstructure was in place and painted Dunkelgelb (dark sandy yellow). When the engine was started and the Nashorn was driven for the first time the whole team were excited and proud of the work that had been accomplished. There was still a lot of work to do. The gun and gun shield had not been fitted at that point. But then disaster struck.

'On Sunday, 10 March, we had a call from a neighbour who lived near the workshop where we kept the Nashorn. He told us that there was a massive fire and the fire brigade had been called. Within 30 minutes, the workshop was completely burned down, and there was extensive, heart-breaking, damage to the Nashorn.

The Nashorn Restoration Project's leader, Robby van Sambeek.

'A lot of the components, internal and external fittings, were beyond repair. Most of the steel parts were salvageable. They would lose some of the strength having been in the fire, but as this vehicle was not a fighting vehicle, that did not matter.

'The suspension leaf springs luckily did not get too hot, so they did not deform. They could be reused. But all the rubber parts, like the rims of the road wheels, just burnt off. It was not just the loss of the parts on the vehicle and the damage caused by the fire that was upsetting, but the workshop was where we kept lots of tools, documents, and spare parts that we needed for the restoration project to continue. Most of those were destroyed, too. It could not be insured as the Nashorn was not a complete vehicle.'

Like a Phoenix rising from the ashes

Due to the fire and rebuild work, the team nicknamed it the Nashorn Phoenix. Robby said the engine and transmission were not original as they would have cost more than £230,000 and the expense of maintaining and running the vehicle would have been prohibitive. Spare mechanical parts would also be difficult to find, and when located, prices exorbitant.

'The final drive steering unit is from a Cold War British FV432 armoured personnel carrier,' he explained. 'The engine and the gearbox are from a Drag-Line crane. The engine is a Deutz FL12814 V12 17-litre 300hp. They are known for their reliability, and spare parts are readily available. This Nashorn was never intended to be a static museum piece. We wanted it to be driven regularly at military history events.'

Top: Refurbished road wheels and wheel arms. Above: Motive power – the Deutz FL12814 V12 17-litre 300hp engine.

Top: Drive sprocket. Above centre: Superstructure in red primer ready for camouflage. Above: Fire damaged road wheels. Below: Newly-cast tracks.

Plans to use the original Second World War tracks were abandoned because the metal was too brittle.

The Nashorn's main armament, the 8.8cm PaK 43/1.

One of the biggest challenges the team faced was fabricating the gun's elevation and traversing mechanisms from scratch.

Several drive shafts have failed due to stress loads from brake steering, but the Project have made stronger ones, because the metal was too brittle.

Fortunately, the metal parts of the road wheels and return rollers were reusable after the fire. 'New rubber rims were made by a company in Poland. They are vulcanised on steel rings and the steel rings are pressed on to the wheels with the aid of some lubrication,' said Robby. 'Hilary Louis Doyle, a trustee of the UK-based Weald Foundation, heard about the fire and arranged for two rubber-rimmed road wheels to be gifted to the project to help us back on the road to recovery. We placed them in the spare wheel racks on the front of the fighting compartment superstructure. It is nice to have friends like that.'

The fire incident was also picked up by volunteers at the Flakpanzer Restoration Project at Base Borden Military Museum in Canada. 'They offered to help and made a 3D CAD model of the rubber rim of a return wheel,' said Robby. 'That was 3D printed and used to form the mould for the casting of the new rubber rims. We also had to make a two-part mould to reproduce the rubber suspension bump stops, as they had all melted in the fire.' Robby said the project team's initial goal was to use original Second World War track links of the same type as a lot of the original track links were included with the purchase, while others were sourced from friends and dealers.

'We did have some problems with the original track links breaking at the point where the upright open "A"-shaped centre guide piece joins the top part of the tread,' he said. 'This seems to have been a poor design and a common casting fault. Later versions of this type of track had a solid, closed upright "A"-shaped centre guide piece to make it much stronger.

'We also lost a track during a drive at the Overloon War Museum. This was also a casting issue. The sockets that hold the track pin in place just fractured. These track links are over 76 years old, and some are fragile.

'A few years ago the Nashorn was put on temporary display at the Overloon War Museum and moving it there also highlighted the track links with cracks. So, they had to be removed, the cracks ground out and if possible, welded.

'A few links with broken centre guide pieces had new "A"-shaped guides welded into place after the remains of the old ones were cut away. The new "A"-shaped guide pieces were salvaged from other unrepairable track links. Some links had to be replaced from the small stock of replacement links.' As a result, the team had to abandon the original plan to use Second World War tracks.

'They were just too brittle,' said Robby. 'We looked at buying a new set of bespoke cast track links from a company in the UK and we have an agreement with the company to test the tracks for them.'

The gun challenge

The biggest challenge the team faced was having to make the gun's elevation and traversing mechanism from scratch. 'We are still looking for original parts, and if they are found, we will replace the fabricated elements,' said Robby. 'The gun cradle system sits on the hull deck that goes over the middle-positioned engine.'

Meanwhile, the protective armoured walls of the fighting compartment have been rebuilt using original parts except for a small piece at the front on the left of the vehicle. 'We used Facebook to ask for help trying to locate missing sections and good friends of the project, like the Australian Armour and Artillery Museum in Cairns, Queensland, Australia, found an original rear right-side hatch door and shipped it to us. "We made some interesting discoveries when measuring the armour thickness. Most of the armour was 10mm thick. The hull armour thickness was 30mm at the front and 20mm at the side and rear. The hull floor was only 15mm thick. This means the crew would only be protected from small arms fire and shrapnel.'

This was because the Nashorn was never designed to be at the front of an attack, engaging enemy armour at close quarters. It was a long-range ambush weapon, ideal for protecting the flanks of an attack or lying in wait in a wood or thick hedgerow for an enemy counterattack. The open top meant the crew were particularly vulnerable in an urban environment from snipers and handheld grenades. There was no protection from airburst artillery shells. The protective armoured driver's cabin had not survived, and the team needed to have a new one made. The hatches are original, as are the hinges of the front hatches.

> **'The Nashorn restoration team ultimately decided they needed to raise funds to finance a set of newly cast tracks that would not fail.'**

A triangular piece of metal was welded in front of the driver's front visor on the glacis plate to replicate the original bullet splash deflector. All the robust metal hinges for the back hatches had to be fabricated along with some brackets, hatch handles and locks. The long-legged 'A'-shaped gun travel lock is still on the list of items to be found or made while the gun shield and the gun shield bottom edge bullet deflector had to be built from scratch.

'We still have to make ammunition boxes and other internal fittings,' said Robby. Lengths of metal rods had to be bent into inverted 'U' shapes. They were welded into

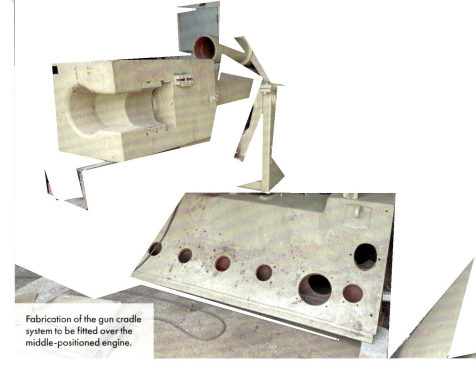

Fabrication of the gun cradle system to be fitted over the middle-positioned engine.

position just below the top of the fighting compartment's armoured exterior walls and some lower down near the top of the hull. Crews would have used these to lash down a tarpaulin that covered the open-top during bad weather. Wire or string would have been tied to them and run up and down and across the outside to enable green vegetation to be strapped to the exterior of the vehicle to help camouflage it. Two lengths of thicker gauge metal rods were bent into shape to form the exterior spare road wheel holders. All the pipework and fittings for the exhaust system also had to be built.

What the future holds

'When we first mentioned that we aimed to sell the Nashorn once completed, we received a lot of negative comments on social media as it was taken out of context,' said Robby. 'We are a non-profit volunteer organisation. We aim to bring back to life as many vehicles to their original state as we can. The proceeds from a future sale of the Nashorn would be used to reinvest in another historical project and restore that back to a working condition, if possible. We want to preserve history so the next generation can learn about it.'

'There are many people we need to thank from the international community of military vehicle restorers, museums and historians for their help and advice on this project and out of the three surviving Nashorns, this is the only one in a working condition.'

Originally published in Classic Military Vehicle *in October 2022 and reproduced here with thanks to Key Publishing.*

HELP THE NASHORN
The Nashorn Restoration team continues to search for original parts. If you would like to help fund future work for this mighty vehicle, visit: www.gofundme.com/f/nashorn-sd-kfz-164-restoration

SPECIFICATION SD.KFZ. 164 NASHORN

Crew	5	Height	2.65m (8ft 8in)	Engine	Maybach HL120 TRM 11.9-litre 296hp V12 petrol
Armament	8.8cm Pak 43/1 gun (main), 1 x 7.92mm MG 34 or MG 42 MG	Ground clearance	0.40m (15¾in)		
		Combat weight	24 tonnes (23.6 tons)		
		Armour	hull: 20–30mm (0.78–1.18in), superstructure: 10mm (0.39in)	Max speed	42kmh (26.71mph)
Length with gun	8.44m (27ft 8in)			Max range	260km (146 miles)
Length hull	6.20m (20ft 4in)			Production	494
Width	2.95m (9ft 8in)				

IN THE ARENA
WORLD WAR TWO: ARMOURED THRUSTS IN NORTH WEST EUROPE

The advance on Germany in 1944-45 was arguably the zenith of armoured warfare. By this stage, experienced units had mastered the numerous means to fight in and against tanks

The museum's Sherman M4A2E8 was the mechanical star of the 2014 film *Fury*. A2 indicates that the vehicle is fitted with the General Motors 6046 12-cylinder twin in-line diesel engine. E8 means it is fitted with the Horizontal Volute Spring Suspension, abbreviated as HVSS and nicknamed the 'Easy Eight' suspension. It is armed with a long 76mm gun and fitted with 'wet' ammunition stowage.

SHERMAN FURY

The Tank Museum's M4A2E8 Sherman *Fury* was built at the Fisher Body Tank Plant in Grand Blanc, Michigan, in March 1945. Its serial number is 65016 and is believed to be one of five of this type supplied to Britain during the Second World War. It came to The Tank Museum in 1985 from the Defence Academy of the United Kingdom at Shrivenham.

In the 2014 Sony film *Fury* it plays the part of the far more common M4A3E8, a type that saw extensive service with the United States Army in North West Europe toward the end of Second World War.

M24 Chaffee *Hemlock III* was fully restored by Armoured Engineering for the Bannister Collection and it has recently returned to The Tank Museum for display.

Above: An Otter Light Reconnaissance Car leads a Humber and a Daimler Armoured Car. Below: Two half tracks – the American M16 anti-aircraft vehicle is trailed by the German Sd.Kfz. 7 artillery tractor. Bottom: M4A2E8 *Fury* is supported by American infantry reenactors.

TANKFEST SOUVENIR SPECIAL **51**

Top: M4A2 *Fury*; above: Daimler Armoured Car; below: 50cal on the turret of M4A2 *Fury*.

Mike and Chris Phelps' M18 Hellcat *Bronx Bruiser* was built by Buick in 1944 and was classed as a tank destroyer. It has an open-topped turret and is equipped with a 76mm gun as main armament with a 50cal as secondary.

'The Buick M18 tank destroyer, *Bronx Bruiser*, made its first TANKFEST appearance in 2022.'

A line up of guest German vehicles is led by the Sd.Kfz. 222 Leichter Panzerspähwagen, followed by an Sd.Kfz. 251 half-track.

ANTI-TANK WEAPONS
'TANK TE PANZERSC

Normandy, late July 1944. Having just shot across a road junction in his Sherman tank, 19-year-old 2nd Lieutenant David Render, Sherwood Rangers, halts outside a white stone cottage in the village of Briquessard a few miles west of Villers-Bocage. 'The Inevitable Mr Render' (as he was nicknamed) takes up the story: 'I reported that I was firm on the radio and was about to call Lane's Sherman forward when a bloody great explosion ripped into the grass bank a few feet to the left of us. The enemy bazooka team was located less than 30yds away in a cottage garden across the green and must have panicked. Their second round was also a miss and went high over my head, shattering the roof of the cottage and showering the tank with slate shards. I was already shouting fire-control orders into the mic before the Germans managed to get their third shot in. Martin traversed the turret to the left, firing the coaxial 30-cal as he went.

'Stamping on the main armament fire button as soon as the turret slewed to a stop, he was spot on with the first HE shell. He swivelled the turret a few inches left to right and hosed the houses down with mg fire. I watched a second round impact among a score of scurrying figures. They were trying desperately to get out of the gardens and escape the heavy weight of fire by running between the houses. But at that range we couldn't miss, and machine-gun bullets and shell fragments cut them down to a man.'

The dead were Fallschirmjäger and Render was surprised they had missed him, but this was the first Panzerschreck attack they had experienced and the Panzerschreck was duly scooped up and sent back to HQ. It was a prize – apparently the first Panzerschreck to be captured by the British in Normandy. Render's recollection of this action not only demonstrates the danger that Allied tank crews faced from Panzerschreck and Panzerfaust ambushes, but it also highlights the deadly cost to German anti-tank teams if they missed their target.

SPECIFICATION
Type Anti-tank grenade launcher
No built 314,895
Variants RPzB 54, RPzB 54/1
Weight 11kg (24lb) empty (RPzB 54 with shield)
Length 164cm (65in)
Calibre 88mm (3.5in)
Muzzle velocity 110m/sec (360ft/sec)
Effective firing range 150m (490ft) RPzB 54
Munition RPzBGr 4322 rocket-propelled grenade

RROR'HRECK

Stuart Wheeler investigates the German Second World War reusable rocket-launched shaped-charge anti-tank weapon called the Panzerschreck – known to its operators as the 'Tank Terror'.

To recognise successful infantry one-man anti-tank kills, the Panzervernichtungsabzeichen decoration was introduced in March 1942, silver for one kill, gold for five. The award was extended to Panzerschreck teams in December 1943, highlighting the danger that they faced. Around 18,450 had been awarded by the end of the war.

Panzerschreck – the 'Tank Terror'

Panzerschrecks started to be slowly issued to troops from October 1943 onwards, equipping dedicated tank-destroyer units and selected infantry divisions. By 1944–45, approximately 83 Panzerschrecks were available per infantry regiment. By late-1944, the defensive-focused Volksgrenadier divisions had eschewed towed anti-tank guns, equipping the division with 72 Panzerschrecks.

Tactically, Panzerschrecks were best employed from concealed positions, targeting the flank or rear of AFVs in ambushes on avenues of approach. Keeping tanks buttoned up and blinded by supporting units using infantry fire, smoke and artillery was crucial in allowing Panzerschreck teams to manoeuvre with Panzerschrecks being carried by sling over the shoulder, or transported distances by horse and infantry cart.

When meeting encounters, the two-man Panzerschreck teams tended to be held in reserve and brought up when needed. Given the fire, smoke, and dust kicked up when firing Panzerschrecks, moving positions after firing was recommended. There is evidence of Panzerschrecks being used in a mortar role at Cassino in 1944, but the advice was that given its limited anti-personnel capability, the focus should be using it to attack tanks.

In defensive situations, Panzerschreck teams were usually deployed in teams of three, two up with one behind, with up to a 150m (165yds) between positions. This allowed teams to cover a front of

A captured Püppchen is tested by a British Army officer.

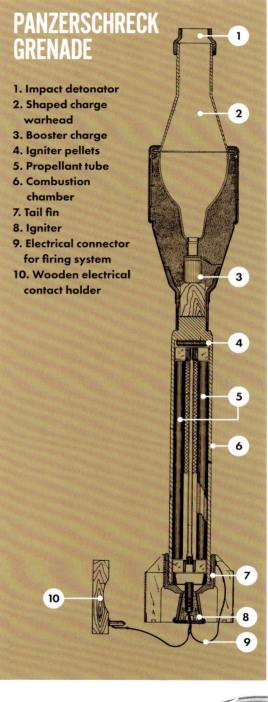

PANZERSCHRECK GRENADE

1. Impact detonator
2. Shaped charge warhead
3. Booster charge
4. Igniter pellets
5. Propellant tube
6. Combustion chamber
7. Tail fin
8. Igniter
9. Electrical connector for firing system
10. Wooden electrical contact holder

450m and 300m (492yds and 328yds) in depth, but this was dependent on suitable terrain and with avenues of approach. Slit trenches were frequently used allowing Panzerschreck teams 360° fields of fire.

Origins in the Raketenwerfer 43 'Püppchen'

With a single-use shaped-charge anti-tank weapon called the Panzerfaust already in development, the Germans looked to produce a second, reusable anti-tank weapon to replace the obsolescent Panzerbüchse 39 anti-tank rifle. What would become one of two direct influences on the development of the Panzerschreck, the Raketenwerfer 43 'Püppchen' (or 'Dolly'), really came down to the design of the ammunition, developed by Dr Erich von Holt, of the Westfalian Anhalt Explosives Stock Company (WASAG). It was the Püppchen's calibre, in this case 8.8cm, which would have a major influence on why the Panzerschreck did not adopt the 60mm size used by the US M1 Bazooka and demonstrated at Kummersdorf in March 1943.

Shortcomings

On the plus side, what the Raketenwerfer offered the infantry was the ability to penetrate 160cm (63in) of homogeneous steel at 500m (547yds) range, for stationary targets, or 230m (252yds) for targets that were moving. But ultimately, the Raketenwerfer was let down by its weight that made it difficult to easily manhandle over rough terrain on the battlefield. For sure, it was significantly lighter than the obsolete 3.7cm (1½in)

A Panzerschreck team in action in Russia during summer 1944. The Panzervernichtungsabzeichen (or tank destruction badge) on the sleeves of both men suggests a successful tank-killing partnership.

German troops dismount from transport with their Panzerschrecks.

'Although the use of a breech eliminated any back-blast, it did produce considerable muzzle flash and obscuration when fired.'

PaK 35/36, but it still weighed a hefty 150kg (328lb) and was awkward to carry, so it was hardly the man portable anti-tank weapon solution which the infantry was looking for. That's despite the ability to break down the 1.6m (5ft 3in)-long rocket projector, carriage, shield, two steel-wheeled rubber tyres or skids and trail into seven individual man-packable loads.

Moreover, although the use of a breech eliminated any back-blast, it did produce considerable muzzle flash and obscuration when fired, and any recoil was transferred directly through the carriage into the ground. Just over 3,000 were manufactured at quite a considerable cost.

From Püppchen to Panzerschreck

Ultimately, as captured examples of the M1 Bazooka began to filter through to German design departments from November 1942 onwards, it was clear that the Püppchen's design was found wanting in comparison, being less efficient and versatile, and a decision was made to develop a similar lightweight launcher tube. Consequently, HASAG, the Hugo Schneider Works, was given the contract to design the Schulder 75 launcher and WASAG the contract to produce an electrical detonator version of the Püppchen's 4312 existing percussion pin and cap-detonated rocket. Basically, the Püppchen's rocket warhead was suitable for use but required a different firing mechanism and longer body, becoming the 4322.

Initially, the new design went under a number of names at the early stages of its development – 'Harvest Wreath', Raketenpanzerbüchse 54 and Ofenrohr (Stovepipe), before receiving its official Hitler-approved name Panzerschreck ('Tank Terror') at the same time, November 1943, as the Panzerfaust. Main Panzerschreck production was undertaken by three firms: Enzinger-Union-Weerke, Schricker and Company, and HASAG Eisen-und Mettallwerke, with the RPzB 54 model being issued to German troops from October 1943 onwards. Almost 315,000 were manufactured before the war's end, with three-quarters of that figure being produced in 1944.

Effectiveness

In terms of effectiveness, the Panzerschreck offered the German infantry a multi-use anti-tank weapon with which to engage targets at longer ranges than the Panzerfaust.

During fighting in Ukraine in spring 1944, a young soldier handles a Pz.BGr. 4322 HEAT rocket used with the Panzerschreck.

TANKFEST SOUVENIR SPECIAL 57

The Raketenpanzerbüchse 54 (Panzerschreck) with blast shield was also nicknamed the 'Ofenrohr' or 'Stovepipe' because of the weapon's large tube and the copious amounts of smoke it produced.

In December 1943, the Panzervernichtungsabzeichen decoration was extended to Panzerschreck teams to recognise successful infantry one-man anti-tank kills – silver for one kill, gold for five. Some 18,450 had been awarded by the war's end.

However, a report by General Heinz Guderian on anti-tank effectiveness in the first four months of 1944 on the Eastern Front indicates that the Panzerschreck was significantly less effective than the Panzerfaust, achieving only one-third of the tank kills attributed to the Panzerfaust – 88 compared to 265. The Panzerschreck was also more wasteful in its kill achievement ratio, requiring over two-thirds more rounds to knock out a tank, that's 1,061 per kill compared to the Panzerfaust's 691. For the Western Allies in North West Europe, the Panzerschreck and Panzerfaust were an increasing threat from the D-Day onwards with kills peaking over 20 per cent in July 1944, and from April 1945 reaching a massive 41 per cent in the final days of fighting.

Panzerfaust or Panzerschreck?

It's possible to guess at why the Panzerfaust may have been more effective than the Panzerschreck. First, they were more widely distributed and easier to conceal, they were less awkward and heavy to carry, and did not produce the same amount of flame and smoke giving their position away. Second, they had a more powerful penetrating capability, 200mm compared to 160mm. Third, they needed to be used at closer ranges meaning there was more chance of gaining a hit. And, finally, they could be used more effectively in volley-firing or tank-stalking scenarios.

To sum up, the Panzerschreck gave the German infantry another multi-use anti-tank capability to replace or supplement the other anti-tank defences at their disposal. It wasn't perfect, given its size and weight, and the tell-tale back-blast, but it was an improvement on the Panzerbüchse 39 and the Püppchen. Ultimately, as a German version of the bazooka, with little in the way of improvements, its post-war legacy didn't last much longer than producing scrap metal for consumer goods and going into storage with the Finns.

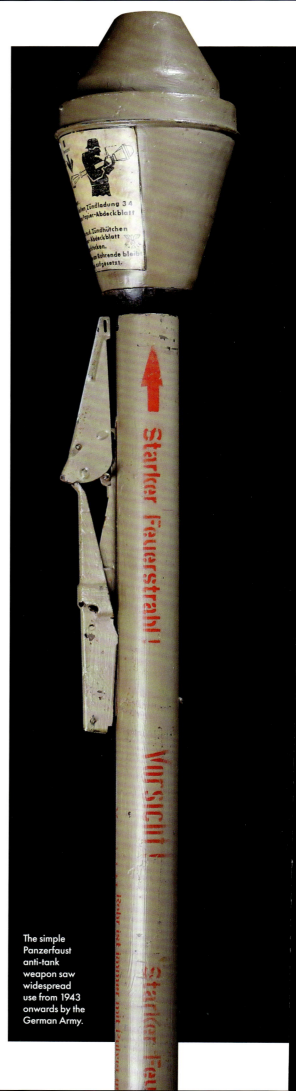

The simple Panzerfaust anti-tank weapon saw widespread use from 1943 onwards by the German Army.

PANZERFAUST CHEAP AND DEADLY

In April 1945, Colonel Roberts of the US 4th Armored Division summed up the Panzerfaust threat: '[It's] the worst weapon we have encountered in this exploitation type of war. It will go through any US tank, and can be handled by even an inexperienced individual. It is the only weapon fighting our tanks today.'

Issued widely, the Panzerfaust was a simple-to-use defensive weapon for German forces as they retreated into the Reich. In Germany, Hitler Youth and Volkssturm or Home Guard units were sent out on bicycles armed with the weapon to ambush advancing Allied tanks.

The 'tank' or 'armour fist' was launched by a single soldier, holding the launch tube under their arm and blasting the warhead forward – depending on the model – to 30, 60, 100 or 150m. The tube that had contained the black powder propellant could then be thrown away. A wooden shaft behind the warhead carried folded, stabilising fins, which sprung out to keep the warhead on a straight flightpath. The hollow charge warhead could penetrate around 200mm of armour plate, which was more than that carried by most Allied tanks.

Wartime trials confirmed the Panzerfaust as the primary choice over Panzerschreck due to its better penetration, and its one-person operation capability. Panzerschreck offered greater range and accuracy but it cost more – 100 Reichsmarks per weapon plus 10 rockets – compared to the Panzerfaust, which was between four to six times cheaper. It is estimated that over eight million Panzerfausts of all types were made before the end of the Second World War.

An army sergeant aims a Panzerfaust 60 using the integrated leaf sight.

A Panzer regiment NCO instructs a boy of the Hitler Youth in the use of the Panzerfaust.

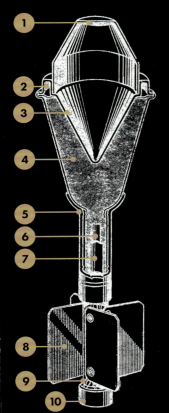

PANZERFAUST HOLLOW CHARGE BOMB

1. Impact cap
2. Steel ring
3. Cavity liner (60° cone)
4. Approx 3lb 7oz CYC/TNT
5. Tail tube
6. Cavity for gaine
7. Cavity for fuse
8. Flexible unpainted steel fins
9. Wooden stem
10. Steel cap.

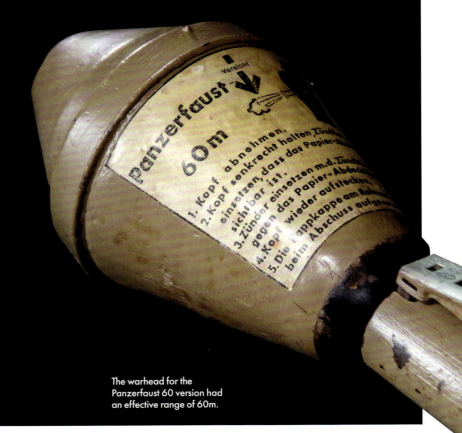
The warhead for the Panzerfaust 60 version had an effective range of 60m.

A 'barn find' is the collectors' Holy Grail: this was the first viewing of the Centaur in Mike Roberts' farm shed where the tank was parked in amongst some hay bales. (*All photos courtesy Armoured Engineering Ltd*)

'Supporting The Tank Museum and seeing vehicles like the Centaur III run at an event like TANKFEST gives me immense pleasure,' says Museum Trustee and military vehicle collector William Bannister.

RESTORATION STORY
RETURN OF THE CENTAUR

Military vehicle collector and The Tank Museum Trustee **William Bannister** talks to **Jonathan Falconer** about his fascination with tanks and the restoration of his latest acquisition, a rare Centaur III.

Awaiting restoration work at Armoured Engineering Ltd. Parked behind the Centaur is the freshly restored M24 Chaffee, which is also part of the Bannister Collection.

'This particular tank starred in the series *Band of Brothers* and I recognised that the Centaur represented a gap in The Tank Museum's collection.'

Preparing to run the Liberty engine and set the ignition timing at Armoured Engineering Ltd's facility in Romney Marsh, Kent.

Above: The clutch assembly on the Liberty V12 engine.

Below: Fitting the engine compartment framework and deck panels.

I believe that supporting a charity should not just be about donating money, but also about giving of your time,' asserts William Bannister, a trustee of The Tank Museum, collector of historic military vehicles, and Chief Executive of Motor Fuels Group, the UK's largest independent forecourt operator.

'I want to contribute in the future to The Tank Museum's active fleet of Second World War armour by adding running vehicles used by the British Army that they may already only have as static exhibits. Supporting the museum and seeing these vehicles run at an event like TANKFEST gives me immense pleasure,' he says.

From a young age, William has had a fascination with tanks. He was taken to The Tank Museum when he was 12 years old by his parents and 'I enjoyed it so much' he recalls, 'that the visit has led to a lifelong interest in it and what it does.'

William was reintroduced to the museum as an adult about 16 years ago. He then volunteered in the Workshop. 'I commuted to Bovington once a month and after a number of years volunteering, I joined the museum's Appeals and Fundraising Boards before being invited to become a trustee. This was a great honour for me,' he discloses.

Acquiring the Centaur

William started his collection with an M3A1 Stuart, the British Army's iconic Western Desert tank, which is an important vehicle in the story of British armour. He then acquired an M24 Chaffee and an M4A4 Sherman, but then the opportunity came up to buy a Centaur, a Mark III that had been converted prior to D-Day from a gun tank to an armoured bulldozer, or 'Dozer'. 'I met Denis and Mike Roberts who owned the vehicle, which had sat gathering dust in their barn for 20 years. Incidentally, this tank also had the claim to fame of having starred in the series Band of Brothers. Denis and Mike were very helpful and I recognised that the Centaur represented a gap in The Tank Museum's collection,' he declares.

'Around 250 of the Centaurs that were produced were converted to Dozers,' explains William, 'but the vehicle started life as a gun tank and not a Dozer. The hull is definitely that of a Centaur III. It's a rare AFV with a Liberty engine and it tells the story of the cruiser tanks, through Cromwell to Centurion.' He continues: 'The Centaur III is also known as the Cromwell IV. The key is it uses the old Liberty engine, which powered all British cruiser tanks at the time. When the Meteor engine replaced the Liberty engine in the Centaur, the tank was designated Cromwell, which is otherwise indistinguishable to the untrained eye,' he points out.

Some 950 or so Centaurs were built and 223 were built as the Centaur III with the 75mm gun. This gun was then standardised in all subsequent Cromwell tanks. 'We don't know the exact detail of where the turret originally came from. We know it came from a range and has suffered quite a bit of damage, but it's certainly the correct turret and gun for the hull,' he says. This will be fully restored as part of the second phase restoration of the vehicle.

Important workshop information for the Centaur III is contained in this official publication from 1945.

The Centaur III had been converted before D-Day from a gun tank to an armoured bulldozer, or 'Dozer'.

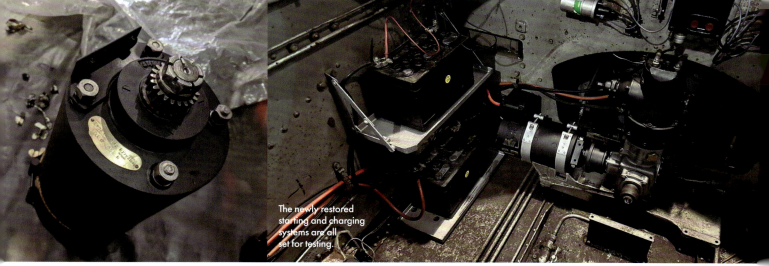

The newly restored starting and charging systems are all set for testing.

A replacement turret was needed for the Centaur and one was duly found on a gunnery range where it had suffered damage, which was skilfully repaired by Armoured Engineering Ltd.

SPECIFICATION
CRUISER TANK MARK VIII
CENTAUR MARK III

Crew	5
Armament	75mm ROQF Mk V
	2 x 7.92mm BESA MG
	2 x Vickers K .303in MG with PLM AA mounting, alternatively BREN
	Smoke mortar, 2in
Length with gun	21ft 0¾in (6.4m)
Length hull	21ft 0¾in (6.4m)
Width	10ft 0in (3.05m)
Height	7ft 8¾in (2.32m)
Ground clearance	15in (0.38m)
Combat weight	24–28 tons loaded (24.38–28.45 tonnes)
Armour, hull	57mm/67° front, 32mm/90° side, 32mm/90° rear, 8mm/0° top/bottom
Engine	V12 395hp Nuffield Liberty petrol
Max road speed	25.36mph (41kmh)
Max road range	165 miles (266km)
Production	233 (most Centaurs I's converted to III's)

'TANKFEST 2023 is the first opportunity to exhibit the Centaur III to the public after a first phase restoration.'

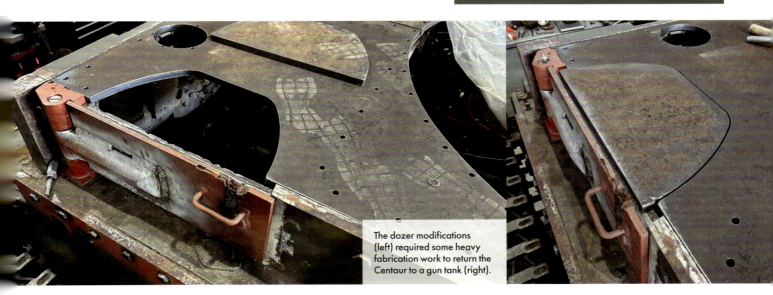

The dozer modifications (left) required some heavy fabrication work to return the Centaur to a gun tank (right).

TANKFEST SOUVENIR SPECIAL **65**

The voltage regulator fully overhauled and returned to service.

It became apparent that the voltage regulator (left and below) required a full overhaul by a specialist. The driver's dash panel (bottom) was also in need of complete restoration.

A passion for AFV restoration

William received help from Track & Wheel at Gawcott in Buckinghamshire who specialise in the restoration, rebuild and servicing of military vehicles. 'They had the Centaur for an initial overview. I also had great help from Denis and Mike Roberts, who have supplied operating manuals and other assistance,' he confirms. 'The company carrying out the full restoration of the vehicle is Armoured Engineering Ltd, located on the edge of Romney Marsh in Kent. It is owned and run by Gavin Barlow who also manages my collection of military vehicles,' reveals William.

'I have worked with Gavin and his team now for over seven years. He has combined his skills as a REME reservist with a passion for historic armoured vehicle restoration, to build a successful and respected business,' he explains. 'Their attention to detail is fantastic and for my collection we take pride in restoring the vehicles to original condition in every way possible.'

William is passionate about restoring vehicles to the highest standard. 'Getting things to work like the rare Liberty and Chrysler Multibank engines is difficult,' he admits, 'but they're so important to the tank story.'

The reason he secured the M4A4 Sherman, or Sherman V in British service, was because out of 7,499 built there are only three left in the world in working order with the Chrysler Multibank engine. This rarity is all the more surprising as it was the most numerous of the M4 series received by the British Empire as Lend-Lease. It was important, therefore, that it was secured for display at The Tank Museum for the public to see and enjoy.

First show for the Centaur

TANKFEST 2023 is the first opportunity to exhibit the Centaur III to the public after a first phase restoration. William is careful to explain that this is only the first phase

The gearbox removed from the hull. This unit enables the Centaur to carry out the neutral turn.

The Centaur's stripped back hull after a full overhaul of the wheel stations and removal of dozer mods.

of a longer restoration process for the Centaur. 'So far, we've done the basics needed to make the vehicle run safely. We've got the Liberty engine running, and Gavin and the team have concentrated on the key mechanical and electrical components that make it safe to use,' he explains.

'The plan is for the tank to stay at the museum until later next year and to run in events like TANKFEST as part of a "shakedown" process. No doubt there will be all kinds of problems that'll need sorting out, but we'll then return the vehicle to Armoured Engineering to be taken apart again for a full restoration inside and outside.

'Restoring 80-year-old vehicles takes a long time and thousands of hours of commitment, but I hope that the public enjoy this early appearance of the Centaur at TANKFEST this year,' he says.

TANKFEST SOUVENIR SPECIAL 67

IN THE ARENA
THE COLD WAR: SUSPICION AND STOCKPILING

As an 'Iron Curtain' fell across Europe, mutual mistrust saw tank development and production continue at pace.

The West German Leopard 1 received a dizzying array of upgrades from its many operators during and after the Cold War. This is a Canadian C2 model, dating from the mid-1990s.

With its distinctive oscillating turret, the French AMX 13 light tank entered service in 1953 and has proved a huge success. Over 7,000 were built for almost 30 countries and it was developed into dozens of variants. It has seen extensive combat, mainly with Israel and India.

'Tank guns and fleets increased in size as superiority of threat was sought – but thankfully never truly tested.'

This ex-Polish Army T-72 Main Battle Tank was exchanged with a Chieftain Mk 11 in 2014, since when the T-72 has become a regular performer in the Kuwait Arena.

The M60A1 was the backbone of the American tank fleet for much of the Cold War (even including into the First Gulf War with the US Marine Corps), and also gave long service to the Israeli Defence Force.

CHIEFTAIN MBT

The Chieftain was a key component of Britain's Cold War army and a highly visible armoured presence on NATO's eastern border in Germany.

It equipped armoured units of the British Army of the Rhine (BAOR) defending West Germany against possible Warsaw Pact attack.

The Chieftain is also a crucial element in the story of both the Royal Armoured Corps and British tank development.

When it entered service as Britain's Main Battle Tank in 1965, the Chieftain was in many ways ahead of its time, but despite a 30-year service life it never fired a shot in anger with British forces.

Of all the tanks in The Tank Museum's collection, none is more numerously represented than the Chieftain. At the time of writing in spring 2023, the museum has 23 Chieftains in total, covering a range of different marks and variants.

Above: This Panzer 57/60 tank, a Swiss Centurion variant, was donated to The Tank Museum by the Swiss Army – Centre for Historic Equipment of the Armed Forces (CHEAF) in 2021. Below: Three of The Tank Museum's Leopard 1s parade around the arena. The leading two are Canadian C2 variants, with the third being a German Leopard 1A1A2 model.

Challenger 1, 34KA11, entered service with the British Army in August 1983, making it one of the earliest of the 420 Challengers built. It was delivered as a Mark 1.

Cold War foes: Soviet T-72 and US M60A1. The T-72 entered Soviet service in 1974 and is the most widely used main battle tank in the world, while the M60 was the standard American tank for most of the Cold War.

TANKFEST

90 SECS WITH
TIM BROAD
COMMENTATOR

'Believe me, having a Chieftain tank hurtle past within a few feet of you and hearing the reaction of a crowded arena is very special,' exclaims Tim Broad, one of TANKFEST's commentators. After retiring from a career in teaching that included history, he volunteered at The Tank Museum, joining the Guide team initially and working with school groups before moving to wider public involvement. 'Shortly after coming to the museum I expressed an interest in commentating on some of the "Tanks in Action" arena displays,' he says.

So, where does Tim's particular interest in tanks come from? 'I'm a Midlander, one of the generation of Britons that grew up with the *Victor* and *Eagle* comics, played on bomb-sites and watched those splendidly stiff-upper-lip British war films in black and white on tiny television screens, so it was almost inevitable that I would become fascinated by military history – a passion that has stayed with me,' he confides. 'The genesis of my particular interest (and modest expertise) in armoured vehicles is, frankly, harder to explain – it always seems to have been there,' he adds. In fact, the signs were evident from an early age as Tim's first school prize was a book on tanks, much to his headmaster's bewilderment.

'To my delight (and no little surprise) the museum gave me the opportunity to commentate – Tiger Day and TANKFEST followed,' he says elatedly.

TANKFEST SOUVENIR SPECIAL **71**

BAT GUN
BATTALION ANTI-TANK RECOILLESS WEAPON

Stuart Wheeler examines how interwar developments of the principle of recoilless rifles led post-war to High Explosive Squash Head (HESH) ammunition and Britain's 120mm Battalion anti-tank (BAT) gun design of 1950s, which transformed the Army's tank-killing potential.

Born out of the Cold War Project Vista, the M50 Ontos mounted six 106mm manually loaded recoilless rifles as its main armament.

The 10.5cm Leichtgeschütz 40, also known as the LG 40, was a German recoilless gun manufactured by Krupp and used during the Second World War.

A contender for one of the oddest post-Second World War designs was the US M50 Ontos. Fitted with six 106mm recoilless rifles, the two-man crewed Ontos was part of an early 1950s US scientific and military Cold-War concept, Project Vista, named after the hotel in which the meeting was initially convened, which envisioned Western Europe being defended by hundreds of infantry strongpoints, anti-tank minefields, and thousands of recoilless rifles mounted on cheap and expendable vehicles. The belief in scientific circles was that the Soviet tank threat could be met by the High Explosive Anti-Tank (HEAT)-firing M40 Battalion anti-tank rifles mounted on the Ontos rather than outdated anti-tank guns, or expensive tanks.

Although the principle of the recoilless rifle had been known for centuries, the origins of its development as a truly useable combat weapon dates back to just before the Great War, when Cleland Davis, a US Navy commander, developed a single-barrel gun that produced no recoil. He achieved this by using two propellant charges, placed back-to-back in the centre

by burning a quantity of propellant gas as it did not matter what came out at the rear of the barrel as long as the recoil was balanced. Put simply, the projectile went one way the gas the other. The key to using propellant gas was to use a venturi, a smaller diameter section that choked the gas, speeding it up, before it was released rearwards through a cone-shaped funnel.

The second important innovation was the design of the propellant case as it needed to contain five times as much propellant as a conventional case to achieve the recoilless effect. To release the propellant rearwards, the base featured an opening to permit the counter-weight gas to flow out. However, propellant will only burn properly under pressure, so the opening was temporarily closed by using a Bakelite bursting disc, which allowed the remaining propellant to kick the projectile towards the target before burning up. A firing cap was included in the centre of the disc.

The Krupp design used a rear-based breech, lightweight carriage, and the use of larger calibre shaped charge shells meant that the low velocity of the gun did not compromise its effectiveness, resulting in the LG40 7.5cm for use as an infantry gun for German airborne units where it made its combat debut in Crete. The Krupp design set the design standard for modern recoilless rifles to come.

Britain's innovator of the recoilless rifle

For the British, the development of the recoilless rifle was largely down to one man: Sir Charles Denniston Burney. Retiring from the Royal Navy as a commander, Burney had been involved with a number of innovations, including the R100 airship, but independently of the Germans he had also started to look at the Davis recoilless principle, initially with a four-bore punt gun. By 1944, Burney had moved on from his initial 20mm anti-tank recoilless design to a larger calibre 3.45in (88mm) one. This gun was viewed as being light enough, at 75lb (34kg), to mount on the shoulder, although images of an upright soldier bracing himself to fire it suggests that this was not the best firing position.

Regarding the ammunition, Burney used a propellant case with perforated sides, employing thin sheet brass to maintain the initial propellant pressure. This set-up allowed

of the barrel, which, when fired, forced a projectile forward, while simultaneously forcing the same weight of buckshot rearwards. Interestingly, the Davis gun was rejected for ground use but saw combat as an aircraft weapon for hunting U-boats, although the operator had to be wary that the buckshot did not damage his aircraft at the same time.

Krupp improves the Davis recoilless principle

While the Davis gun is remembered now more as a curiosity, the work done by Krupp designers in 1930s Germany was key to improving the Davis recoilless principle. Looking for a lighter infantry support gun, capable of firing a large calibre round, the Krupp designers realised that the buckshot could be replaced

A soldier shoulders the 3.45in Burney–Weeks recoilless rifle.

The Land Rover fitted with the WOMBAT could carry six HESH rounds.

TANKFEST SPECIAL **73**

the gas to vent sideways from the case and exit through four venturis, although this design was found to be more susceptible to gas erosion than the single venturi iteration.

Squash head ammunition

However, the most innovative part of the design was the use of a high explosive shell to attack armour. This employed what became known as the squash head principle. Basically, what happens is that when the warhead hits the target, a quantity of HE deforms and spreads in contact with the armour and is detonated via a base fuse. This sends a high velocity compressive shock wave travelling through the armour plate until it reaches the interior air behind the plate. On contact with the air, the wave is reflected back towards the initial detonation and more primary shockwaves. It is the meeting of these two waves that causes the shockwaves to combine, creating a reinforced shockwave, which is what overmatches the strength of the plate, subsequently detaching a large metal scab from the rear of the armour. This detached 'scab' moves at between 30 and 130m/sec and will be around 25 to 50 per cent larger than the diameter of the High Explosive Squash Head (HESH) warhead. The HESH round could have a massive concussive effect and break external and internal fittings such as vision devices and sights. The impact of a 150mm (5.9in) slab of metal would be devastating on the tank crew inside.

Birth of the 120mm BAT gun

With the end of the Second World War, the need to replace the 6pdr and the 17pdr anti-tank guns had become urgent. Burney's subsequent recoilless designs, such as the 3.7in (94mm) gun's lightweight carriage, had proved unsuitable, but his 4.5in (114mm) recoilless close-support gun introduced a stronger carriage and the fitting of a steel shield.

By 1946, Burney, under the auspices of his Broadway Trust Company Limited, had designed a 4.7in (120mm) recoilless gun, with which he was investigating the use of rocket-assisted ammunition and for which the Ordnance Board had ordered 80 rounds. It was this design that became the basis for the 120mm Battalion anti-tank (BAT) gun design of 1950. The key improvements were the adoption of the Krupp LG 40 single venturi mounted on the breech block and the use of a plastic bursting disc in the base of the propellant case. Ignition was achieved through a special band located in the propellant case. Entering service in 1953, the first L1 120mm BATs were a bit on the heavy side, with the gun weighing in at 1,000kg (0.98 tons), but they were still a third of the weight of the 17pdr and had a smaller profile even with the shield. Despite its relatively lighter weight, it was a difficult weapon for the three-man crew to manhandle. Concerns about the BAT's weight saw a number of improvements introduced to the L2 BAT series with the lightened Modified BAT, or MOBAT, dropping the shield and traversing gear, which helped to reduce the weight by almost a quarter, permitting the MOBAT to be used in a towed role behind a Land Rover.

Enter the WOMBAT

The last iteration of the 120mm L6 BAT design arrived in service in 1964: the WOMBAT or Weapon of Magnesium. Interestingly, the origins of the WOMBAT's name have also been linked to with that of the Australian marsupial, but it is difficult to confirm if this was indeed the case. It also received a non-official sobriquet the 'VC gun'

Above: With the gunner's eye firmly fixed on a target, the two remaining members of this MOBAT crew are ready to reload with another 120mm HESH round. Note the gun is traversed to fire over the wheels.

HESH ROUND AND PROJECTILE

1. Inert filling
2. Shell body
3. Explosive main filling RDX/TNT
4. Base fuze
5. Driving band
6. Cup
7. Tracer No 30
8. Propellant
9. Cartridge case
10. Igniter, RCL cartridge.

from its crews, as the voluminous back-blast would tend to give their position away once it had been fired. Anyway, what we do know is that the WOMBAT used lightweight magnesium alloys in the carriage and high-grade steel in the barrel, reducing the weight by over 60 per cent from the MOBAT to a very svelte 295kg (650lb). Dimensionally, the WOMBAT also showed this weight loss, shrinking by 43 per cent to 85cm (33½in) in width, as well as reducing its height, which was helped by the reduction in the WOMBAT's wheel diameter by 23cm (9in). It also featured a new rotating ring lock breech, which swung open to the right. One of the key reasons for this weight-saving was that the WOMBAT was designed to be carried portee in a long wheelbase Land Rover rather than towed, and therefore the wheels and carriage did not need to be as robust.

Basically, the WOMBAT was an attempt to make the recoilless gun more mobile, at a time (the late 1950s) when the infantry was aware of the dangers of the atomic battlefield and how being encumbered by weapons that required towing would impact on their mobility. The solution came via the Infantry's Trials & Development Wing who, by 1967, had devised a simple six-bolt mount for the WOMBAT so it could be operated directly from inside the FV 432. Some 118 of these mounts were produced and could carry 12 rounds; the Land Rover could carry 6. Six WOMBATs in three sections were the typical organisation for the Anti-Tank Platoon.

Before this mounted capability, the firing of WOMBAT and the other BAT variants, the infantry weapons teams were encouraged to fire from prepared gun pits. However, the requirements for a Battalion anti-tank gun

Hand ready on his trigger, this WOMBAT gunner uses his telescopic sight to identify a target and engage.

'The WOMBAT was 60 per cent lighter than the MOBAT so it could be carried portee in a Land Rover.'

had changed by the late 1970s/early 1980s and the WOMBAT was becoming more obsolete as the increasing use of guided anti-tank weapons, as well as short-range man-portable recoilless weapons such as the 84mm Swedish Carl Gustav began to dominate the anti-tank scene. WOMBAT was used by the Australians, and MOBAT was used by Jordan, Kenya, Malaysia and New Zealand. Along with a BAT and WOMBAT example, The Tank Museum is fortunate to have an L7 CONBAT, an upgraded converted BAT.

Below right: By mounting the WOMBAT on FV432s, the infantry were able to use the carrier's mobility and protection to manoeuvre their recoilless guns on the nuclear battlefield.

THE BRITISH ARMY AND THE FUTURE OF THE TANK

Against a demonstration of power by the Royal Armoured Corps (RAC) we explain why the tank is as relevant now as it ever was – and that it will be so for years to come.

The Supacat MWMIK/Jackal is a patrol and reconnaissance vehicle designed to protect personnel against roadside explosions and mine attack.

CHALLENGER 2 'MEGATRON'

'Megatron' is a Challenger 2 Main Battle Tank based at the British Army's Combat Manoeuvre Centre at Bovington in Dorset. It is operated by the Armoured Trials and Development Unit. ATDU uses 'Megatron' for the trialling of new and possible future equipment for all British Army Challenger 2 tanks. The name 'Megatron' is a nickname given to the vehicle after a character in the science fiction action films franchise *Transformers*. The latest version of 'Megatron' is fitted with a combination of reactive, passive and bar armour that provides unique protection against new threats on the modern battlefield.

The Challenger Armoured Repair and Recovery Vehicle (CRARRV) is designed to repair and recover damaged tanks on the battlefield. It has two winches and a hydraulic crane capable of lifting and carrying a complete Challenger 2 power pack.

Titan (third vehicle in) is an armoured bridgelayer (AVLB) based on the Challenger 2 MBT chassis. It can lay a selection of close support bridges, with the longest being the 32m No 10 bridge.

'Megatron' has been a regular attendee at TANKFEST since 2016.

Armed with the 30mm Rarden cannon, Warrior is an Infantry Fighting Vehicle that is also used for reconnaissance by the Armoured Cavalry regiments of the Royal Armoured Corps.

The Jackal 2's general armament includes a 7.62mm GPMG and either a .50cal HMG or grenade machine-gun (GMG) as the main weapon system. It is an ideal platform for reconnaissance, rapid assault, fire support and convoy protection. The vehicle has a crew of three and a range of 500 miles (800km).

'The Mobility Weapon-Mounted Installation Kit (MWMIK), or 'Jackal', is a high mobility weapons platform used by the Light Cavalry regiments of the Royal Armoured Corps.

Foxhound incorporates cutting edge vehicle technology and provides unprecedented levels of blast protection for its size and weight.

TANKFEST SOUVENIR SPECIAL **79**

ANTI-TANK WEAPONS
NLAW
THE ULTIMATE TANK KILLER

Tanks have traditionally enabled crews to hunt their prey in relative safety, but as **Stuart Wheeler** reveals, the shoulder-launched NLAW is turning the tables by removing this safety level, attacking a tank from above, and earning it the soubriquet of the 21st century's ultimate tank killer.

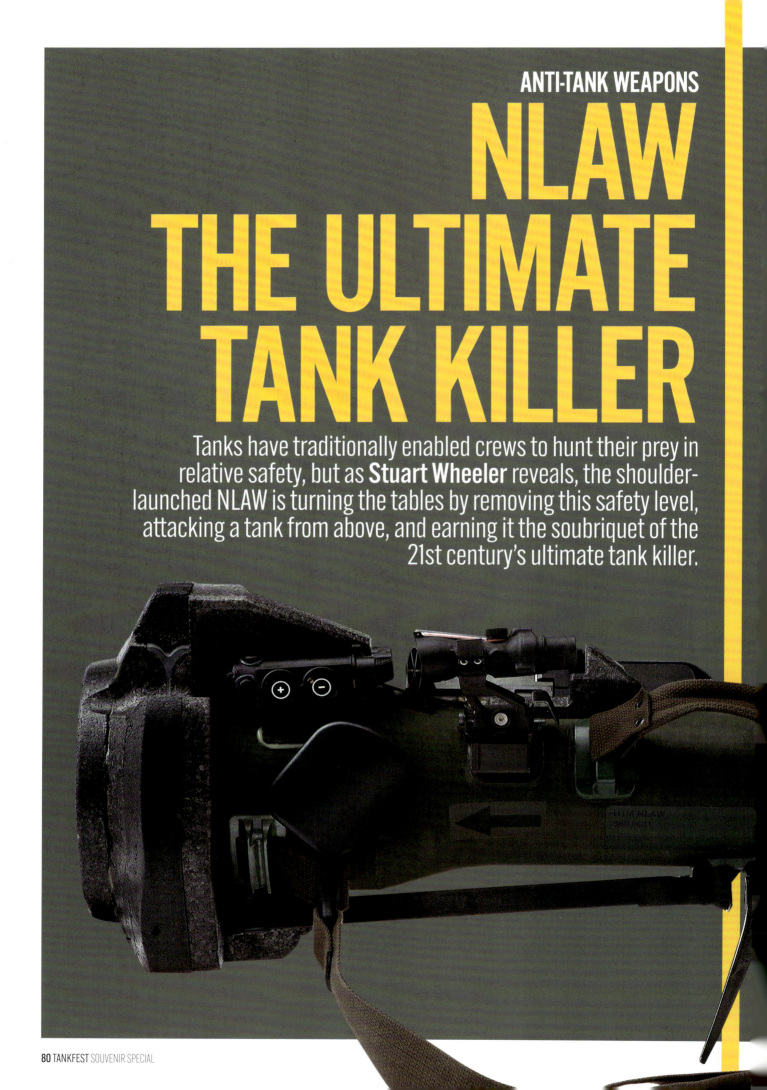

It's interesting how certain weapons enter the general public's consciousness to reach an iconic status. You have your Maxim and Vickers machine-guns, and tanks from the Great War. Your Tigers, Shermans, Jeeps and Bazookas from the Second. Your AK-47s, M16s, RPGs and of course nukes from the post-war period. The Next Generation Light Anti-tank Weapon, or NLAW, may be joining the likes of the IED (Improvised Explosive Device) as a 21st century culturally iconic weapon, with Boris Johnson even being asked to sign one on a recent visit to Ukraine.

Of course, prior to 2022, few people outside military circles, or military interest groups, would really have been aware of the NLAW's existence. However, Russia's invasion of Ukraine has raised the NLAW's profile to an international audience awed to see daily videos of how brave individuals, carrying a smart anti-tank weapon, can stalk, target, engage and ultimately knock-out Russian tanks while escaping to fight another day.

Genesis

So, what are the specific origins of the NLAW? The acronym LAW – Light Anti-Armour Weapon – really starts back in the early 1960s with the US Army's adoption of the M72 LAW – a short-range 66mm unguided shoulder-launched anti-tank weapon, which really fed into the post-war need for a portable, anti-tank weapon that a single soldier could use. There have been updates – the NLAW's direct predecessor, the Insys LAW 80 for instance – offered approximately 700mm (28in) of armour penetration but was still unguided and did not have a top-down-attack capability, limiting its penetration against heavy armour, although utilising a bigger 94mm (3.7in) warhead as well as a 9mm (0.35in) spotting rifle was an improvement.

NLAW – the first ever non-expert, single-shot, short-range, anti-tank missile system able to knock out any main battle tank, in any situation, from any angle and in any environment.
(Cpl Danny Houghton RLC/ UK MOD © Crown Copyright 2021)

With this in mind, the UK's Staff Requirement (Land) 4098 specified that what was needed was a generational update that could provide individual soldiers with a Light Anti-Armour capability with which to defeat modern reactive armour-equipped AFVs in confined spaces in urban envi-ronments. By May 2002, a decision had been made. This saw the Lockheed Martin, MBDA and Insys' Team Kestrel bid, with its Predator-based system, developed for the US Marine Corps, losing out to the MBT LAW, developed by the Swedish firm Saab Bofors Dynamics AB. This late-1990s design featured a top-down-attack weapon, which utilised existing mature technologies, namely a warhead, guidance, fuse, the ability to fire in confined spaces and insensitive munitions derived from both the BILL 2 – Bofors Infantry Light & Lethal (my favourite anti-armour acronym) – and the AB AT-4 anti-tank weapons, which had also been developed by Bofors.

SPECIFICATION

Typical combat range
20–600m

Max firing range
1,000m

Main target
MBT (all aspects)

Operation
Single-soldier
Guided/ballistic
Predicted line-of-sight
(fire-and-forget)

Night vision capability
NVS (Thermal Imager and Image Intensifier) goggles compatible

Disposable weapon
Yes.

The one-man portable NLAW (Next Generation Light Anti-tank Weapon) has the power and tactical advantage within close combat to effectively destroy the most advanced MBT with just one shot, striking it from above. (www.saab.com)

TANKFEST SOUVENIR SPECIAL 81

A Gunner with an Armoured Infantry Battlegroup carries a Next Generation Light Anti-Tank Weapon (NLAW) during a live firing exercise on the Salisbury Plain training area. (*Stuart Hill © Crown Copyright*)

Fire-and-forget

Interestingly, the Staff Requirement didn't specifically identify the need for a fire-and-forget capability. The term 'Fire-and-Forget' gets bandied about a lot with later generations of anti-tank weapons. Basically, what we are talking about is the ability of the missile to lock on and travel to a target without the operator still having to command it – that is, to steer it directly – onto the target. In essence, fire-and-forget is really a modern update on earlier unguided anti-tank systems, which allows the operator to move once the missile has launched thereby reducing the chance of the operator being hit by counter-fire.

In terms of size, the NLAW is just over one metre long – interestingly about the same length as a Second World War Panzerfaust. Its use of composite materials means that it has managed to keep the weight down to an impressive 28lb (12.7kg).

The NLAW is a short-range weapon, which has two arming distances – 20m or 100m (66ft or 328ft). This allows the operator to target close, or more distant targets, out to 600 to 800m (1,968ft to 2,625ft).

In terms of engagement, the NLAW operator has the choice of two attack angle modes. The OTA or Overfly Top-Attack, which is the default mode, is used to engage moving targets from above, targeting their weakest armour, and is identified with an orange strip. In direct attack mode, it can be used to engage static targets or those where OTA can't be utilised

Warheads

In its original form the MBT LAW featured two shaped charge warheads, a precursor and main, positioned in the missile to fire vertically downwards as the missile flew above the target. This was also a feature of the tandem warhead on the BILL 2, the precursor being designed to take out any explosive reactive armour, but

> '*In terms of size, the NLAW is just over one metre long – interestingly, about the same length as a Second World War Panzerfaust.*'

82 TANKFEST souvenir special